Getting into
Medical
School
2011 Entry

Getting Into guides

Titles in this series

Getting into

Medical School

2011 Entry

Steven Piumatti

15th Edition

trotman | **t**

Getting into Medical School: 2011 Entry

This 15th edition published in 2010 by Trotman Publishing, an imprint
of Crimson Publishing Ltd, Westminster House, Kew Road, Richmond,
Surrey TW9 2ND

© Joe Ruston 1996; Joe Ruston and James Burnett 1998, 2000, 2001,
2002, 2003, 2004, 2005, 2006; James Burnett 2007, 2008; Steven
Piumatti 2009, 2010

Previously published by Trotman & Co Ltd

Author: Steven Piumatti

British Library Cataloguing in Publication Data
A catalogue record for this book is available from the British Library

ISBN 978-1-84455-237-5

Typeset by IDSUK (DataConnection) Ltd
Printed and bound in the UK by TJ International Ltd, Padstow, Cornwall

Contents

About the author

Steven Piumatti is a Director of Studies and Careers Advisor at Mander Portman Woodward. He is in charge of the Medical programme and runs work experience and interview preparation programmes for potential medics and medical students. He has also written the *Getting into Dental School* guide.

Acknowledgements

In order to write this book, I have needed help from many sources. Without the help of the medical schools' admissions departments, this book would not exist, and I would like to record my gratitude to all of the people who gave up their time to answer my questions. I am very grateful to Miranda Birkby, James Burnett and Dr John Wright in particular for their help. Finally, I would like to thank the students who have provided me with interview questions, factual material and encouragement.

Steven Piumatti
January 2010

For up-to-date information on medicine and medical schools, go to www.mpw.co.uk/getintomed

About this book

First of all, a note on terminology. Throughout this guide, the term 'medical school' includes the university departments of medicine. Second, entry requirements have been quoted in AS and A level terms; a general guide to the grades or scores that you need if you are taking Scottish Highers, the International Baccalaureate or other qualifications can be found on page 1.

This book is divided into nine main chapters, which aim to cover three major obstacles which would-be doctors may face:

- getting an interview at medical school
- getting a conditional offer
- getting the right A level grades.

The nine chapters discuss the following:

1| the study of medicine
2| preparation and getting an interview
3| the interview stage and getting an offer
4| results day
5| non-standard applications
6| careers opportunities
7| fees and funding
8| current issues
9| further information.

Chapter 1 gives information on the actual study of medicine and then beyond, such as possible specialisations and post-degree options. Chapter 2 deals with the preparation that you will need to undertake in order to make your application as irresistible as possible in order to get an offer and/or an interview. It includes advice on work experience, how to choose a medical school and the mechanics of the UCAS application process.

Chapter 3 provides advice on what to expect at the interview stage, and how to ensure that you come across as a potential doctor, whilst Chapter 4 looks at the options that you have at your disposal on results day and describes the steps that you need to take if you are holding an offer or if you have been unsuccessful and have not been given an offer. What then are your possible next steps?

Chapter 5 is aimed primarily at overseas students and any other 'non-standard' applicants – mature students, graduates, students who have studied arts A levels and retake students (most medical schools consider non-standard applicants). The chapter also includes some advice for those who want to study medicine outside the UK, say, for example, in the US.

Chapter 6 touches on career options in medicine, while Chapter 7 will give some information regarding fees and funding, and possible bursaries and scholarships.

Chapter 8 presents some key information on contemporary and topical medical issues, such as NHS reforms and genetic engineering. Knowing about medical issues is a must, particularly if you are called in for an interview.

Finally, in Chapter 9, further information is given in terms of further reading. A number of other excellent books are available on the subject of getting into medical school. Furthermore, the contact details of the various medical groups and universities can be found here.

The difference between other guides on getting into medical school and this one is that this guide is a route map; it tells you the path to follow if you want to be a doctor.

To that extent it is rather bossy and dictatorial. I make no apologies for this because I have seen far too many aspiring medical students who took the wrong subjects, who didn't bother to find work experience and who never asked themselves why they wanted to be a doctor before their interview. Their path into medicine was made unnecessarily difficult because they didn't prepare properly.

Throughout the book you will find case studies and examples of material that will reflect to some extent the theme being discussed at that point. I hope that you find these real-life examples illuminating.

Finally, the views expressed in this book, though informed by conversations with staff at medical schools and elsewhere, are my own, unless specifically attributed to a contributor in the text.

Introduction

A realistic chance

Approximately two out of every five students applying for entry to medical school gain a place. Many of those who are rejected are excellent candidates with good GCSE results, high predicted A level grades and a genuine belief that medicine was the right career for them. So why are they unsuccessful? Clearly, not everyone who wants to become a doctor can get into medical school as there are a fixed number of places available. However, many good candidates do not give themselves a realistic chance of getting an interview because their preparation is not as thorough as it ought to be. If you are to prepare effectively for your application, you need to start early – ideally two years before you are due to submit it to UCAS. However, even in a short period of time (a few months), you can put together a convincing application if you follow the advice in this book.

According to the latest available statistics from UCAS on entries and applicants for the 2008 application cycle intake into medical schools there was a 8% increase on applicants compared with the 2007 numbers.

By the October deadline in 2009, UCAS had received 15,181 applications for medical school places from UK students and a further 3,626 applications from international students. Therefore in 2009, nearly 19,000 students were battling for the 8,000 places that are available at UK medical schools.

Table 1 gives some comparisons and data on the 2008 application cycle.

The grades you need

Table 8 (pages 134–5) shows that, with a few exceptions, the A level grades you need for medicine are AAA. You might be lucky and get an offer of ABB, but you won't know that until six months before the exams, so you can't rely on it. Some medical schools now require AAA. As a general guide, candidates offering qualifications other than A levels are likely to need the following:

- Scottish: ABB in Advanced Highers
- International Baccalaureate: around 35 points including 6, 6, 5 at Higher Level (including Chemistry)

Table 1 2008 application cycle data

Category of applicants	Numbers of applicants	Accepted places
Age 17–19 (UK only)	9740	5356
Age 20–29 (UK only)	4424	1617
Age 30+ (UK only)	540	149
Age 40+ (UK only)	133	22
All men	8129	3504
All women	10431	4519
All EU (except UK)	1692	228
All non-EU	2030	653

Source: www.ucas.co.uk/about_us/stat_services/; www.ucas.co.uk/about_us/stat_services/stats_online/annual_datasets_to_download/
Note: 2009 application statistics were not available at the time of going to press.

- European Baccalaureate: minimum of about 70% overall, with at least 80% in Chemistry and another Full Option science/mathematical subject.

But there's more to it than grades …

If getting a place to study medicine was purely a matter of achieving the right grades, medical schools would demand AAA at A level (or equivalent) and 10 A* grades at GCSE, and they would not bother to interview. However, to become a successful doctor requires many skills, academic and otherwise, and it is the job of the admissions staff to try to identify who of the thousands of applicants are the most suitable. It would be misleading to say that anyone, with enough effort, could become a doctor, but it is important for candidates who have the potential to succeed to make the best use of their applications.

■ Non-standard applications

Not all successful applicants apply during their final year of A levels. Some have retaken their exams, while others have used a gap year to add substance to their UCAS application. Again, it would be wrong to say that anyone who reapplies will automatically get a place, but good candidates should not assume that rejection first time round means the end of their career aspirations.

Gaining a place as a retake student or as a second-time applicant is not as easy as it used to be, but candidates who can demonstrate genuine commitment alongside the right personal and academic qualities still have a good chance of success if they go about their applications in the right way. The admissions staff at the medical schools tend to be extremely helpful and, except at the busiest times of the year when they simply do not have the time, they will give advice and encouragement to suitable applicants.

Admissions

The medical schools make strenuous efforts to maintain fair selection procedures: UCAS applications are generally seen by more than one selector, interview panels are given strict guidelines about what they can (and cannot) ask, and most make available detailed statistics about the backgrounds of the students they interview. Above all, admissions staff will tell you that they are looking for good 'all-rounders' who can communicate effectively with others, are academically able and are genuinely enthusiastic about medicine – if you think that this sounds like you, then read on!

Reflections of a doctor

The words below from a qualified practitioner and then from a mature student embarking on a career in medicine express and reflect some of the many challenges and rewards that you also may face in your own journey to become a doctor. Like every journey, the grandest ones start with the first minuscule step.

There is a true joy in qualifying as a doctor. All the hurdles of getting into medical school and the midnight oil burnt to pass the countless exams are behind you, and for the first time in our life you have the honour of putting the initials 'Dr' in front of your name. It's better than being knighted.

However, your journey through medicine is only just beginning. Ahead of you lie more hurdles and the difficult choices of what field to specialise in.

Anyone considering medicine will understand the rewards of medicine: the privilege of caring for others and being let in to their most private world; the opportunity to be an advocate for the most vulnerable in society; the respect that comes from being in the most trusted profession; the variety of work; the intellectual challenge; and the chance to work in a team of like-minded individuals.

There are many challenges as well. All new doctors will need to sub-specialise, and that requires more exams. Gaining the experience to become a good doctor requires putting in the hours, day and night. Expectations are ever higher and consumer demands can lead to difficult consultations and litigation. While making people better can be heart warming, making mistakes or seeing people become sicker and die can be heart wrenching.

One of the early decisions to make is whether to become a general practitioner or a hospital doctor. The first phase in your career is to gather all the knowledge and skills required to become certified in your chosen area. The second is to build on your experience and confidence, and often to sub-specialise in discrete clinical areas. The third stage is to act as a mentor and leader of more junior colleagues. All three stages provide the chance to develop interests in education, research or medical management.

Medicine is a broad church that accommodates varied brethren, from the compassionate to the technical, the intellectual to the practical. There is one theme that is common to all: the desire to improve the well-being of individuals and communities. While the work can be stressful, and the responsibility can sometimes be crushing, being a doctor will always be occupying and fulfilling.

Dr John Wright

Director of Clinical Governance and Operations Medical Director at Bradford Royal Infirmary

Patrick is a genetics graduate who is now studying A level Chemistry over a year. He currently holds four offers subject to his receiving an A grade in the June examinations.

Patrick writes:

> Medical school is a completely different world. It gives you a very accurate reflection of what life in the profession will be like, stressful but uniquely absorbing at the same time.

This is a mature reflection on a course that is the same for students of any age. For any student who has an intention to study this course, preparations should have begun long ago. You cannot fail to appreciate the importance of work experience and how much of a role that will play in your acceptances. In my interviews, work experience was called into question and the experiences I learnt from them were dissected (excuse the pun) at great length. If nothing else, work experience confirms whether this is the right choice of career for you, and believe me, from experience, you have to be sure.

That is the best piece of advice that I can give any student: know what you want and work for it. Any problems, ask. The more contact you have with an admissions tutor, the more they will believe that you are dedicated to what you wish to achieve. You cannot be expected to know everything and therefore people do not mind being asked questions. Blagging in this career is never advisable!

Many people I know have applied for a similar career, some have got in, others – and really able candidates – have not, simply because they have not convinced the interviewer that they have thought through every aspect of this course. Be true to yourself, it is a hugely rewarding career, but in order to help others, you must really want to do it.

01 Studying medicine

This chapter mainly discusses studying medicine as an undergraduate course. For information on postgraduate courses, see the section entitled 'Postgraduate courses' on page 12.

Medical courses are carefully planned by the General Medical Council (GMC) to give students a wide range of academic and practical experience, which will lead to final qualification as a doctor. The main difference between medical schools is the method of teaching. At the end of the five-year course, students will – if they have met the high academic standards demanded – be awarded a Bachelor of Medicine or Bachelor of Medicine and Surgery (referred to as an MB or an MB BS respectively). Many doctors come out with an MB ChB – it all depends on which medical school you go to. Like dentistry, the ChB, i.e. Honours, is largely an honorary title. The MB is the Bachelor of Medicine while the ChB is the Bachelor of Surgery from the Latin *Baccalaureus Chirurgiae*.

It is well worth noting that, at this stage, doctors are graduates and have yet to do (if they so wish) a postgraduate doctoral degree such as a PhD. So they are, in the academic and philosophic sense, not doctors. However, when doctors specialise, it is then necessary to have a post-doctoral degree.

Teaching styles

The structure of all medical courses is similar, with most institutions offering two years of pre-clinical studies (often undertaken with dentistry students at the same university) followed by three years of clinical studies. However, schools differ in the ways in which they deliver the material, so it is very important to get hold of, and thoroughly read, the latest prospectuses of each university you are thinking of applying to.

Medical courses basically fall into three different categories of style:

1| problem-based learning (PBL)
2| traditional
3| integrated (PBL and traditional).

Problem-based learning

PBL is a new and vibrant style of course, which has been commended by the GMC. It was pioneered by medical schools such as Liverpool and Manchester and subsequently taken up by a number of other medical schools such as Barts (Queen Mary), East Anglia, Hull York Medical School, Keele, Peninsula and Sheffield. The course is taught with a patient-orientated approach. From Year 1 onwards, students are heavily involved in clinical scenarios, with the focus on the student to demonstrate self-motivation and proactive self-directed learning. This type of teaching/learning is designed to get away from the previous traditional 'spoon-fed' approach; therefore, those who are used to the spoon feeding of information may take some time to adjust.

Traditional

This is the more long-established lecture-based style, using didactic methods. The majority of these courses are subject-based ones, where lectures are the most appropriate ways of delivering the information. It has to be said that these courses are a rarity today and are perhaps limited to establishments such as Oxford, Cambridge and St Andrews, where there is a definite pre-clinical/clinical divide and the pre-clinical years are taught very rigidly in subjects.

Integrated

Integrated courses are those where basic medical sciences are taught concurrently with clinical studies. Thus, this style is a compromise between a traditional course and a PBL course. Although these courses have patient contact from the start, there is huge variation in the amount of contact from school to school. In Year 1, contact is quite often limited to local community visits, with the amount of patient contact increasing as the years progress. In any case, most students are quite happy with only having limited contact with patients in the first year, as they feel that at this point they do not have a sufficient clinical knowledge base to approach patients on the wards.

■ Differences in teaching style

The main differences in teaching style are usually between patient-orientated, PBL courses and traditional courses which take in the pre-clinical phase, usually in the first two years of the undergraduate degree. In addition, a course may be taught with an emphasis on a specific subject base such as anatomy or biochemistry, or with an emphasis on specific systems-based learning such as the respiratory system or the cardiovascular system. A course may also be integrated, with some aspects of clinical study running alongside the teaching of basic medical sciences. 'Clinical' teaching is similar for all three types of course, and is based in the hospital or in primary care, with teaching for small groups undertaken by clinicians. It is important that you look into the different courses on offer – read the prospectuses and look on the internet before you apply.

Here are two descriptions of a degree in medicine, one from the University of East Anglia (UEA), the other from the University of Nottingham. The first one, from the UEA, seems to have a more systems-based approach, while both offer clinical studies from the outset.

Course structure, University of East Anglia 2010

Our curriculum is characterised by:

- the integration of learning around presentations – rather than by individual discipline or speciality (e.g. anatomy, cardiology) – grouped in system-based units
- the use of clinical settings to pull together core classroom learning – students have clinical contact from the outset of the programme
- the use of primary care as a core setting to show the range of common conditions and normal variation throughout the programme
- student-centred learning
- reflective practice
- predetermined learning outcomes that are shared with students
- group work as preparation for multidisciplinary team working.

The five-year programme

Year 1

- Unit 1: Being a Patient, Being a Doctor (15 weeks)
- Unit 2: Locomotion (15 weeks).

Year 2

- Unit 3: Blood and Skin (12 weeks)
- Unit 4: Circulation (12 weeks)
- Unit 5: Respiration (12 weeks).

Year 3

- Unit 6: Homeostasis and Hormones (12 weeks)
- Unit 7: The Senses (12 weeks)
- Unit 8: Digestion and Nutrition (12 weeks).

Year 4

- Unit 9: Reproduction (14 weeks)
- Unit 10: Growth and Development (14 weeks)
- Unit 11: Elective (8 weeks).

Year 5

- Unit 12: The Mind (14 weeks)
- Unit 13: Emergency Care (14 weeks)
- Unit 14: Preparation for PRHO (5 weeks).

Source: www.uea.ac.uk

Course structure, University of Nottingham 2010

About this course

The medicine course is a five-year degree course. You will acquire the knowledge, skills and behaviour to allow you to graduate with the Bachelor of Medicine and Bachelor of Surgery (BM BS) degrees and to practise as a new doctor on the Foundation training programme. In addition, all students on the five-year course obtain a Bachelor of Medical Sciences (BMed Sci) degree after three years.

Special features of the course

The University of Nottingham is very popular with students wanting to be doctors. Its reputation comes from a number of factors built on a number of features of the course.

- Students have access to excellent facilities within the Medical School offering innovative educational methods. Much of the course relies on e-resources for teaching and assessment.
- There is early interaction with patients starting within the first few weeks of the course. This early patient contact occurs through visits to GP surgeries and hospital wards. During the clinical phases, students have access to five teaching hospitals in the region offering expertise in all the major clinical specialties. Our Clinical Skills laboratory enables students to practise their practical skills throughout the course.

Source: www.nottingham.ac.uk

The reason why a medical course lasts five years is that the teaching covers a wide variety of elements. The pre-clinical students will typically study some, or all, of the following courses: anatomy, biochemistry, biomedical sciences, first aid, oral biology, pharmacology, physiology and an introduction to the clinical skills that will be taught later in the course. In addition, students will cover the effects of anaesthetics and other components common to medicine and dentistry. Furthermore, aspects of psychology will also be considered, due to the fact that as a doctor you will be working in close proximity with people and will be using skills and techniques to relax patients.

Intercalated degrees

Students who perform well in the examinations at the end of their pre-clinical studies (Year 2 or 3) often take up the opportunity to complete an intercalated degree. An intercalated degree gives you the opportunity to incorporate a further degree (BSc or BA) into your medical course. This is normally a one-year project, during which students have the opportunity to investigate a chosen topic in much more depth, producing a final written thesis before rejoining the course. Usually, a range of degrees are available to choose from, such as those from the traditional sciences, i.e. biochemistry, anatomy, physiology, or in topics as wide as medical law, ethics, journalism and/or history of medicine.

- Anatomy continues to be taught using whole body dissection.
- Students will complete two degrees over the five years: the Bachelor of Medical Sciences (in Year 3) and the medical degrees (Bachelor of Medicine, Bachelor of Surgery) in Year 5.
- The research component of the BMed Sci degree provides students with excellent experience in research, with the opportunity of publishing papers.
- A professional approach is taken to training in that it uses procedures that are employed in the assessment of doctors after they graduate.
- The clinical training component of the course sees the amalgamation of students from the Year 4 and 5 courses, which enhances the educational experience for both groups.

Why intercalate?

- It gives you the chance to study a particular subject in depth.
- It gives you the chance to be involved in research or lab work, particularly if you are interested in research later on.
- It gives you an advantage over other candidates if you later decided to specialise; for example, intercalating in anatomy would be useful if you wish to pursue a career in surgery.

Why not intercalate?

- The main drawback is the extra cost and time involved in taking a detour in your studies. This needs to be considered carefully.
- You could forget some of the things you've learnt in the previous years of your medical degree, and thus will need to spend time reacquainting yourself with the forgotten material.

▓ Taking an elective

Towards the end of the course there is often the opportunity to take an elective study period, usually for two months, when students are expected to undertake a short project but are free to travel to any hospital or clinic in the world that is approved by their university. This gives you the opportunity to practise medicine anywhere in the world during your clinical years. For example, electives range from running clinics in developing countries to accompanying flying doctors in Australia. Students see this as an opportunity to do some travelling and visit exotic locations far from home before they qualify. You can also, if you want, opt to do an elective at home. If you want to know more about this, go to www.worktheworld.co.uk/placements/medical_electives.php.

▓ Postgraduate courses

There is a huge variety of opportunities and courses for further postgraduate education and training in medicine. This reflects the array of possible areas for specialisation. Medical schools/hospitals run a wide range of postgraduate programmes, which include further clinical and non-clinical training and research degree programmes.

Advice and guidance are available from the Royal College of Physicians (RCP) (www.rcplondon.ac.uk/college/edu/edu_UCLpgcourses.htm) and the individual universities. As before, you will need to check the prospectuses of individual universities for the most up-to-date information.

Table 2 shows examples of postgraduate courses available, taken from the Manchester University website.

Table 2 Examples of postgraduate courses at University of Manchester

Cancer Studies – Research	Imaging Sciences
Cardiovascular Medicine	Maternal/Fetal Health
Clinical Neurosciences	Medical Education Research
Dermatological Sciences	Medical Genetics
Endocrine Sciences	Occupational and Environmental Health
Epidemiology	Primary Care
Gastrointestinal Sciences	Psychiatry
Genomic Epidemiology	Respiratory Medicine
Health Methodology	Tissue Injury and Repair

Source: www.mhs.manchester.ac.uk/postgraduate/

02 Getting an interview

Getting an interview is essential because most medical schools only issue conditional offers after their admissions panel has met you. The evidence that the selector uses when he or she makes the choice to call you for interview or reject you is your UCAS application. Some sections of the application are purely factual (your name, address, exam results, etc.). There is also a section where you enter your choice of medical schools. The personal statement section gives you an opportunity to write about yourself, and there is a space for your teacher to write a reference describing your strengths and weaknesses. Later in this book, you will find advice on how to fill in these sections and how to influence your referee, but first let's consider what happens, or might happen, to your application.

Typically, a medical school might receive 2,500 UCAS applications, almost all of which will arrive in September and October. The applications are distributed to the selectors, who have to decide which applicants to recommend for interview. The selectors will usually be busy doctors, and the task of selecting promising candidates means a good deal of extra work for them, on top of the usual demands of their full-time jobs. Most of the candidates will have been predicted grades that will allow them to be considered, but the medical school can only interview, perhaps, 25% of them.

A high proportion of applicants will have good GCSE and AS results and predicted grades at A level of ABB or higher, and will have undertaken some voluntary work or work-shadowing. In order to decide who should be called for interview, the selectors will have to make a decision based solely on the information provided by you and your school. If you are not called for interview, you will not be offered a place at that medical school. If your UCAS application does not convince the selector that you are the right sort of person to be a doctor, he or she will reject you. However outstanding your personal qualities are, unless your UCAS application is convincing, you will not be called for interview. This part of the guide is designed to maximise your chances of getting the interview even under the worst circumstances.

Deciding where to apply

There are 32 medical schools or university departments of medicine in the UK. They offer a range of options for students wishing to study medicine:

- five- or six-year MB BS or MB ChB courses (UCAS codes A100 or A106)

- four-year accelerated graduate-entry courses (A101 or A102)
- six-year courses that include a 'pre-med' year (A103 or A104).

Entry requirements of all medical schools are summarised in Table 8 (pages 134–5).

Although you can apply to five institutions, you may only apply to four medical schools; if you enter more than four, your UCAS application will be rejected. The question is: what should you do with the other slot? The medical schools will assure you that you can apply for other, non-medical courses without jeopardising your application to medicine, but I would advise you to think carefully before doing so, for the reasons given below.

- There's no point in thinking about alternatives if you really want to become a doctor.
- If you are unlucky and receive no conditional offers for medicine, you could feel obliged to accept an offer from your 'insurance' course.
- You might find it harder to convince your interviewers that you are completely committed to a career in medicine if you appear to be happy to accept a place to study, say, chemical engineering or archaeology.

The one reason to put a non-medical choice on your form is if you are not prepared to wait a year if your application is unsuccessful, and you intend to enter medicine as a graduate (see page 68).

So, you need to select four medical schools. In deciding which ones to eliminate, you may find the following points helpful.

- **Grades and retakes.** If you are worried that you will not achieve AAB/ABB grades the first time round, include at least three schools that accept retake candidates (see Table 8, pages 134–5). The reason for this is that if you make a good impression at interview this year, you may not need to face a second interview at your next attempt. You will also be able to show loyalty by applying twice to the same school. Many medical schools will consider second-time applicants only if they applied to them originally.
- **Interviews.** A few medical schools do not interview A level candidates. If you think that you will be a much stronger candidate on your application form than in person, it may be advantageous to include these schools. Each school's interview rates are shown in Table 7 (pages 132–3).
- **Location and socialising.** You may be attracted to the idea of being at a university rather than at one of the London medical schools that are not located on the campuses of their affiliated universities. One reason for this may be that you would like to mix with students from a wide variety of disciplines and that you will enjoy the intellectual and social cross-fertilisation. The trouble with this theory is that

medical students work longer hours than most other students and tend to form a clique. Be warned: in reality you could find that you have little time to mix with non-medics.

■ **Course structure.** While all the medical schools are well equipped and provide a high standard of teaching, there are real differences in the way the courses are taught and examined. Specifically, the majority offer an integrated course in which students see patients at an early stage and certainly before the formal clinical part of the course. The other main distinction is between systems-based courses, which teach medicine in terms of the body's systems (e.g. the cardiovascular system), and subject-based courses, which teach in terms of the fundamental subjects (anatomy, biochemistry, etc.) (see page 134 onwards).

■ **Teaching style.** The style of teaching can also vary from place to place. In particular, some medical schools use problem-based learning (PBL) extensively. For example, the course at UEA features PBL, and the programme offers a variety of formats to encourage learning, including whole-class discussions, lectures, seminars and, especially, small-group sessions. Clinical, communication and IT skills are taught throughout. Within each year, clinical experience is provided in general practice and in hospitals. Assessment is on a unit-by-unit basis and includes: multiple-choice questionnaires; portfolios, presentations and projects; 'advance notice' questions in which researched answers are presented under examination conditions; and Objective Structured Clinical Examinations (OSCEs). These are matters of personal preference.

■ **Intercalated degrees and electives.** Another difference in the courses offered concerns the opportunities for an intercalated Honours BSc and electives. The intercalated BSc scheme allows students to tack on one further year of study either to the end of the two-year pre-clinical course or as an integrated part of a six-year course. Successful completion of this year, which may be used to study a wide variety of subjects, confers a BSc degree qualification. Electives are periods of work experience away from the medical school and, in some cases, abroad.

■ Applying to Oxbridge medical schools

Oxbridge is in a separate category because, if getting into most medical schools is difficult, entry into Oxford and Cambridge is even more so (the extra hurdles facing students wishing to apply to Oxford or Cambridge are discussed in *Getting into Oxford & Cambridge*, another guide in this series). The general advice given here also applies to Oxbridge, but the competition is intense, and before you include either university on your UCAS application you need to be confident that you can achieve three A grades at A level and that you will interview well.

You should discuss an application to Oxford or Cambridge with your teachers at an early stage.

You cannot apply to both Oxford and Cambridge in your application and your teachers will advise you whether to apply to either. You would need a good reason to apply to Oxbridge against the advice of your teachers and it certainly is not worth applying on the 'off chance' of getting in. By doing so you will simply waste one of your valuable four choices. You should consult the prospectus of each medical school in your own school's careers library. Once you have narrowed the choice down to about 10 or 12, it is worth writing to all those on your list for a copy of their prospectus (these will be sent to you free of charge) and taking a good look at their websites.

What the selector looks for

Most medical schools use a form that the selector fills in as he or she reads through your application. Have a look at the example form given in Figure 1; the next part of the chapter will examine each heading on this form in more detail.

Academic ability

GCSE results: points total and breadth of subjects

By the time you read this you will probably have chosen your GCSE subjects or even taken them. If you have not, here are some points to bear in mind.

- Medical school selectors like to see breadth. Try to take as many GCSE subjects as possible. Try to take at least eight, but if your school places restrictions on the choice or number of GCSEs you take, make sure this fact is referred to in your reference.
- You will almost certainly need to study two science/maths subjects at A level, and you will need to study chemistry. There is a big gap between GCSE and A level. If you have the choice, don't make that jump even harder by studying combined or integrated science rather than the single science subjects. If your school will not allow you to study the single subjects, you should consider taking extra lessons during the summer holiday after your GCSE exams.
- Medical school selectors look at applicants' GCSE grades in considerable detail. Many medical schools ask for a 'good' set of GCSE results. What does this mean? Well, it varies from university to university, but a minimum of five A/B grades plus a good grade in English Language GCSE is likely to be required. Most medical schools will require higher than this. Some medical schools specify the grades that they require, whilst others use the points

MEDICAL INTERVIEW SELECTION FORM

Name: UCAS number:
Age at entry: Gap year?:
Selector: Date:

SELECTION CRITERIA COMMENTS

1| Academic (score out of 10)
GCSE results/AS grades/A level predictions
UKCAT/BMAT result

2| Commitment (score out of 10)
Genuine interest in medicine?
Relevant work experience?
Community involvement?

3| Personal (score out of 10)
Range of interests?
Involvement in school activities?
Achievements and/or leadership?
Referee supports application?

Total score (maximum of 30):

Recommendation of selector: Interview   Score 25–30
                               Reserve list   Score 16–24
                               Rejection   Score 0–15

Further comments (if any):

Figure 1 Sample candidate selection form

system (see www.dcsf.gov.uk/performancetables for more information).

■ If you have already taken your GCSEs and achieved disappointing grades, you must resign yourself to working exceptionally hard from the first day of your A level course. You will also need to convince your UCAS referee that the GCSE grades are not an indicator of low grades at A level, so that this can be mentioned in your reference.

AS levels: do they matter?

Under the current AS and A level system, there is a lot of pressure on you from the start of your two-year courses since not only do the AS level grades appear on your application, but also many of the medical schools will specify minimum grade requirements. Even those that don't will consciously or subconsciously use them as an indicator of your likely A level grades. Imagine the situation: the selector has one more interview slot to fill, and has the choice between two students with identical work experience, GCSE results and A level predictions; but one scored DDDD at AS level, and the other achieved AAAA. Who do you think will get the place? The other thing to bear in mind is that a score of DDDD is unlikely to lead to AAB at A level since an AS contributes to 50% of the total A level marks, and so the selectors may doubt that the predicted grades (see below) are achievable.

You must be aware of the importance of retaking AS units if possible. Every extra mark gained on the (easier) AS units is a mark that you don't have to get in the (harder) A2 exams. If you have a second attempt at an AS unit, the board will take the higher of the two marks.

A level predictions

Your choice of A levels

You will see from Table 8 (pages 134–5) that most medical schools now ask for just two science/maths subjects at A level, with another science at AS level. They all require chemistry and/or biology so you need to choose either physics or mathematics if you wish to apply to a medical school that requires three science/maths subjects. There are three important considerations.

1| Choose subjects that you are good at. You must be capable of an A grade. If you aren't sure, ask your teachers.
2| Choose subjects that will help you in your medical course; life at medical school is tough enough as it is without having to learn new subjects from scratch.
3| While it is acceptable to choose a non-scientific third AS or A level that you enjoy and which will provide you with an interesting topic of conversation at your interview, you should be careful not to choose subjects such as art, which is practical rather than academic. General studies is not acceptable either. However, students who can cope with the differing demands of arts and sciences at A level have an advantage in that they can demonstrate breadth.

So what combination of subjects should you choose? In addition to chemistry/biology and another science at A level, you might also consider subjects such as psychology, sociology or a language at AS level. The point to bear in mind when you are making your choices is that you need high grades, so do not pick a subject that sounds interesting, such as Italian, if you are not good at languages. Similarly, although an AS level in Statistics might look good on your UCAS application, you will not do well at it if you struggled at GCSE Mathematics. You will need to check the individual requirements, but in general it is likely that most medical schools will prefer at least one AS level to be in an arts or humanities subject.

Taking four A levels
There's no harm in doing more than three A levels or four AS levels, but you should drop the fourth/fifth subject if there is any danger of it pulling down your grades in the others. Medical schools will not include the fourth A level in any conditional offers they make.

The prediction
The selector will look for a grade prediction in the reference that your teacher writes about you. Your teacher will probably make a prediction based on the reports of your subject teachers, your GCSE grades and, most importantly, on the results of the school exams and AS levels that you take at the end of Year 12.

Consequently, it is vital that you work hard during the first year of A levels. Only by doing so will you get the reference you need. If there is any reason or excuse to explain why you did badly at GCSE or did not work hard in Year 12, you must make sure that the teacher writing your reference knows about it and includes it in the reference. The most common reasons for poor performance are illness and problems at home (e.g. illness of a close relation or family breakdown).

The bottom line is that you need to persuade your school that you are on track for grades of at least ABB. Convincing everyone else usually involves convincing yourself!

Aptitude tests

UKCAT
Twenty-six medical schools in the UK require applicants to sit the UK Clinical Aptitude Test (UKCAT). The institutions that require UKCAT are Aberdeen, Brighton and Sussex, Cardiff, Dundee, Durham, East Anglia, Edinburgh, Glasgow, Hull York, Imperial (graduate entry), Keele, King's, Leeds, Leicester, Manchester, Newcastle, Nottingham, Oxford (graduate-entry medical degree), Peninsula, Queen Mary, Queen's Belfast, St Andrews, St George's, Sheffield, Southampton and Warwick.

There is also the UKCATSEN (Special Educational Needs) which is a longer version of the UKCAT for candidates who require special arrangements.

For 2009 entry, the test lasted two hours and assessed aptitude rather than academic achievement. The test comprised five sections:

1| verbal reasoning
2| quantitative reasoning
3| abstract reasoning
4| decision analysis
5| non-cognitive analysis.

You register for the test online at www.ukcat.ac.uk – the site also contains details about the test content and practice tests. Unlike other entrance tests, UKCAT is sat before you apply. You will sit the test at an external test centre – there are 150 test centres in the UK and many overseas. At the time of writing, registration dates for the 2010 test were not available but it is thought these will be similar to the dates for the 2009 test. Registration for the 2009 test (for applicants applying for 2010 entry) started in the first week of June 2009 and ended on 31 August 2009. Applicants had to take the test before the deadline of 10 October 2009, a few days before the deadline for medical applications.

In 2009 the test cost £60 for candidates taking the test in the European Union (EU) before 31 August 2009 and for all other candidates the cost was £95. If candidates took the UKCAT test between 1 September and 9 October 2009, the cost was £75 for candidates taking the test in the EU.

The medical schools use the test scores in different ways: some will specify a minimum mark; others will call the top scorers only for interview; whilst others will use the score alongside all of the other entrance criteria as an extra piece of evidence.

Although the UKCAT website tries to discourage students from doing any preparation for the test other than sitting the practice test available on the website, students who sat the test in the past found that the more practice they had on timed IQ-type tests, the better prepared they felt. In the reference section of most bookshops there are a number of books that contain practice questions of a similar type to the UKCAT. Some useful titles are listed on the website that accompanies this book (www.mpw.co.uk/getintomed).

BMAT
Students applying to study medicine at Cambridge, Imperial (undergraduate entry), Oxford and UCL are required to sit the BioMedical Admissions Test (BMAT). The test, which takes place in November, consists of three sections:

1| aptitude and skills (60 minutes – 35 multiple-choice or short-answer questions)

2| scientific knowledge and applications (30 minutes – 27 multiple-choice or short-answer questions)

3| writing task (30 minutes – one from a choice of three short essay questions).

Sample BMAT question

BMAT Specimen Paper

Section 1 Aptitude and Skills Question 3

Doctors in Great Britain can work for the public health service, a commercial service, or both. 30% of doctors in Great Britain work, at least some of the time, for the commercial sector. On the basis of this information alone, deduce which of the following statements are true of doctors in Great Britain.

1| Some doctors work only in the public health service.
2| More doctors work in the public health service than the commercial sector.
3| Some doctors spend more time on commercial work than in the public health service.

A 1 only
B 2 only
C 1 and 2 only
D 2 and 3 only
E 1, 2 and 3

Answer on page 33

From the specimen papers available on the Cambridge Assessment website (www.admissionstests.cambridgeassessment.org.uk). Reprinted by permission of the University of Cambridge Local Examinations Syndicate.

Further details can be found on www.bmat.org.uk.

■ Commitment

Have you shown a genuine interest in medicine?

This question has to be answered partly by your reference and partly by you in your personal statement but, before we go on, it's time for a bit of soul-searching in the form of a short test, found below. Get a piece of paper and do this immediately, before you read on.

The *Getting into Medical School* genuine interest test

Answer all the questions truthfully.

- Do you regularly read the following for articles about medicine?
  - ☐ daily broadsheet newspapers
  - ☐ *New Scientist*
  - ☐ *Student BMJ*
  - ☐ www.bbc.co.uk/health.
- Do you regularly watch medical dramas and current affairs pro-grammes such as *Panorama* or *Newsnight*?
- Do you possess any books or CD-ROMs about the human body or medicine, or do you visit medical websites?
- Have you attended a first-aid course?
- Have you arranged a visit to your local GP?
- Have you arranged to visit your local hospital in order to see the work of doctors at first hand?
- What day of the week does your favourite newspaper publish a health section?
- Do you know the main causes of death in this country?
- Do you know what the following stand for?
  - ☐ GMC
  - ☐ BMA
  - ☐ NICE
  - ☐ AIDS
  - ☐ SARS
  - ☐ MMR
  - ☐ MRSA
  - ☐ H5N1.

Marking the test

You should have answered 'yes' to most of the first six questions and should have been able to give answers to the last three. A low score (mainly 'No' and 'Don't know' answers) should make you ask yourself whether you really are sufficiently interested in medicine as a career. If you achieved a high score, you need to ensure that you communicate your interest in your UCAS application. The chapter will soon go on to explain how, but first a note about work experience and courses.

'When I read a personal statement, I am looking for a structured account of the journey the student has taken from his or her first idea about studying medicine, outlining the steps taken to investigate what a career in medicine involves. Structure and thorough research make much more of an impact than an "interesting" opening sentence. I am also looking for evidence that the student is a team-player, that he or she takes an active role in extracurricular activities either in or out of school, and can demonstrate situations

*where communication with others is necessary. Closing statements,
however well written, emphasising the student's commitment to
medicine and his/her desire to contribute to the life of the medical
school simply waste space that could be used to discuss work
experience or voluntary work.'*

Admissions Tutor

Have you done relevant work experience and courses?

In addition to making brief visits to your local hospital and GP's surgery
(which you should be able to arrange through your school or with the
help of your parents), it is important to undertake a longer period of
relevant work experience. If possible, try to get work experience that
involves the gritty, unglamorous side of patient care. A week spent helping elderly and confused patients walk to the toilet is worth a month in
the hospital laboratory helping the technicians to carry out routine tests.
Unfortunately, these hospital jobs are hard to get, and you may have to
offer to work at weekends or at night. If that fails, you should try your
local hospice or care home.

Hospices tend to be short of money because they are maintained by
voluntary donations. They are usually happy to take on conscientious
volunteers, and the work they do (caring for the terminally ill) is particularly appropriate. Remember that you are not only working in a hospital/
hospice in order to learn about medicine in action. You are also there to
prove (to yourself as well as to the admissions tutors) that you have the
dedication and stomach for what is often an unpleasant and upsetting
work environment. You should be able to get the address of your
nearest hospice from your GP's surgery or online.

Because of health and safety regulations, it is not always possible to
arrange work experience or voluntary work with GPs, in hospitals or in
hospices. The medical schools' selectors are aware of this but they will
expect you to have found alternatives.

Volunteer work with a local charity is a good way of demonstrating your
commitment as well as giving you the opportunity to find out more about
medicine. HIV/AIDS charities, for example, welcome volunteers. A
spokesman for Positive East, the leading HIV/AIDS charity in East
London, says:

*'Volunteers play an essential role in delivering services, providing
project support, raising essential funds and are central to the
charity's operation. Volunteer roles are tailored to match individual
needs and full training and support is provided. Research and work
placements are also available.'*

Contact details for Positive East can be found at the end of this book.

Any medical contact is better than none, so clerical work in a medical environment, work in a hospital magazine stall or voluntary work for a charity working in a medical-related area is better than no work experience at all. When you come to write the personal statement section of your UCAS application you will want to describe your practical experience of medicine in some detail. Say what you did, what you saw and what insights you gained from it. As always, include details that could provide the signpost to an interesting question in your interview.

For example, suppose you write: 'During the year that I worked on Sunday evenings at St Sebastian's Hospice, I saw a number of patients who were suffering from cancer and it was interesting to observe the treatment they received and watch its effects.' A generous interviewer will ask you about the management of cancer, and you have an opportunity to impress if you can explain the use of drugs, radiotherapy, diet, exercise and so on. The other benefit of work in a medical environment is that you may be able to make a good impression on the senior staff you have worked for. If they are prepared to write a brief reference and send it to your school, the teacher writing your reference will be able to quote from it.

Always keep a diary

During your work experience, keep a diary and write down what you see being done. At the time, you may think that you will remember what you saw, but it could be as long as 18 months between the work experience and an interview, and you will almost certainly forget vital details. Very often, applicants are asked at interview to expand on something interesting on their UCAS application. For example:

> **Interviewer:** I see that you observed a coronary angioplasty. What does that involve?
>
> **Candidate:** Er.
>
> **Interviewer:** Well, I know it's hard to see what's happening but I'm sure you understand the reason for carrying out a coronary angioplasty.
>
> **Candidate:** Um.

Don't allow this to happen to you!

The only problem with work experience is that it can be hard to persuade members of a busy medical team to spend time explaining in detail what they are doing and why. MPW (Mander Portman and Woodward school group) and Medlink and Future Doctors (see page 121) run courses for sixth-formers to help them understand the common areas of medicine and to link this theoretical knowledge to practical procedures.

Have you been involved in your local community?

A career in medicine involves serving the community, and you need to demonstrate that you have something of the dedication needed to be a good doctor. You may have been able to do this through voluntary jobs in hospitals or hospices. If not, you need to think about devoting a regular period each week to one of the charitable organisations that cares for those in need.

The number of organisations needing this help has increased following the government's decision to close some of the long-stay mental institutions and place the burden of caring for patients on local authorities. Your local social services department (their address should in the phone book) will be able to give you information on this and other opportunities for voluntary work. Again, it is helpful to obtain brief references from the people you work for so that these can be included in what your teacher writes about you.

Getting the relevant work experience and courses

It is important to research into why medicine is indeed the right career choice for you. If you have chosen medicine for the wrong reasons, it is likely to come out at interview. There are short courses run by M&D Experience and practising doctors at local hospitals who give an insight into medicine as a career. They do not intend to promote or glamorise medicine, but rather expose it as a profession. This might be an excellent way to assess your motivation at an early stage and also act as part of your work experience in medicine, which would be a good talking point at interview to justify your career choice. See www.mdexperience. co.uk.

▇ Personal qualities

Have you demonstrated a range of interests?

Medical schools like to see applicants who have done more with their life than work for their A levels and watch TV. While the teacher writing your reference will probably refer to your outstanding achievements in his or her reference, you also need to say something about your achievements in your personal statement. Selectors like to read about achievements in sport and other outdoor activities such as the Duke of Edinburgh's Award Scheme. Equally useful activities include Young Enterprise, charity work, public speaking, part-time jobs, art, music and drama.

Bear in mind that selectors will be asking themselves, 'Would this person be an asset to the medical school?' Put in enough detail and try to make it interesting to read.

Here is an example of a good paragraph on interests for the personal statement section:

> I very much enjoy tennis and play in the school team and for Hampshire at under-18 level. This summer a local sports shop has sponsored me to attend a tennis camp in California. I worked at the Wimbledon championships in 2007. I have been playing the piano since the age of eight and took my Grade 7 exam recently. At school, I play in the orchestra and in a very informal jazz band. Last year I started learning the trombone but I would not like anyone except my teacher to hear me playing! I like dancing and social events but my main form of relaxation is gardening. I have started a small business helping my neighbours to improve their gardens – which also brings in some extra money.

And here's how not to do it:

> I play tennis in competitions and the piano and trombone. I like gardening.

But what if you aren't musical, can't play tennis and find geraniums boring? It depends when you are reading this. Anyone with enough drive to become a doctor can probably rustle up an interest or two in six months. If you haven't even got that long, then it would be sensible to devote most of your personal statement to your interest in medicine.

WARNING!

- Don't copy any of the paragraphs above onto your own UCAS application.
- Don't write anything that isn't true.
- Don't write anything you can't talk about at the interview.
- Avoid over-complicated, over-formal styles of writing. Read your personal statement out loud; if it doesn't sound like you speaking, rewrite it.

Have you contributed to school activities?

This is largely covered by the section on interests, but it is worth noting that the selector is looking for someone who will contribute to the communal life of the medical school. If you have been involved in organising things in your school, do remember to include the details. Don't forget to say that you ran the school's fundraising barbecue or that you organised a sponsored jog in aid of disabled children if you did so. Conversely, medical schools are less interested in applicants whose activities are exclusively solitary or cannot take place in the medical school environment. Don't expect to get much credit for:

> My main interest is going for long walks in desolate places by myself or in the company of my MP3 player.

Have you any achievements or leadership experience to your credit?

Again, the main points have been covered already, but you should recall that the selectors are looking for applicants who stand out and who have done more with their lives than the absolute minimum. They are particularly attracted by excellence in any sphere. Have you competed in any activity at a high level or received a prize or other recognition for your achievements? Have you organised and led any events or team games? Were you elected as class representative to the school council? If so, make sure that you include it in your personal statement.

To what extent does your referee support your application?

The vital importance of judicious grovelling to your referee and making sure that he or she knows all the good news about your work in hospitals and in the local community has already been explained. Remember that the teacher writing your reference will rely heavily on advice from other teachers too. They also need to be buttered up and helped to see you as a natural doctor. Come to school scrupulously clean and tidy. Work hard, look keen and make sure you talk about medicine in class. Ask intelligent, medicine-related questions such as those given below.

- Is it because enzymes become denatured at over 45°C that patients suffering from heat stroke have to be cooled down quickly using ice?
- Could sex-linked diseases such as muscular dystrophy be avoided by screening the sperm to eliminate those containing the X chromosomes that carry the harmful recessive genes from an affected male?

Your friends may find all this nauseating – ignore them.

If your referee is approachable, you should be able to ask whether or not he or she feels able to support your application. In the unlikely case that he or she cannot recommend you, you should consider asking if another teacher could complete the application; clashes of personality do very occasionally occur and you must not let the medical schools receive an application form that damns you.

Mechanics of the UCAS application

You will receive advice from your school on how to complete a UCAS application, and you may also find it helpful to consult the MPW guide *How to Complete Your UCAS Application* (see page 122 for details). Some additional points that apply chiefly to medicine are set out below.

Presentation

The vast majority of applications are now completed electronically through the UCAS website using the Apply system. The online system has many useful built-in safety checks to ensure that you do not make mistakes.

Despite the help that the electronic version provides, it is still possible to create an unfavourable impression on the selectors through spelling mistakes, grammatical errors and unclear personal statements. In order to ensure that this does not happen, follow these tips.

- Read the instructions for each section of the application carefully before filling it in.
- Double-check all dates (when you joined and left schools, when you sat examinations), examination boards, GCSE grades and personal details (fee codes, residential status codes, disability codes).
- Plan your personal statement as you would an essay. Lay it out in a logical order. Make the sentences short and to the point. Split the section into paragraphs, with headings such as 'Work experience', 'Reasons for choice', 'Interests' and 'Achievements'. This will enable the selector to read and assess it quickly and easily.
- Ask your parents, or someone who is roughly the same age as the selectors (over 30), to cast a critical eye over your draft, and don't be too proud to make changes in the light of their advice.

The personal statement

When your UCAS application is received by the medical school, it will not be on its own but in a batch, possibly of many. The selectors will have to consider it, along with the rest, in between the demands of other aspects of their jobs. If your application is badly worded, uninteresting or lacking the things that the selector feels are important, it will be put on the 'reject without interview' pile. A typical medical school might receive well over a thousand applications and even more. Table 7 on pages 132–3 shows the numbers that applied for the 2009 year at each of the medical schools. The number of applicants at each university has to then be reduced to 300 or so of which some will be called to interviews. You can only be called for interview on the basis of your

UCAS application. The selectors will not know about the things that you have forgotten to say, and they can only get an impression of you from what is in the application. I have come across too many good students who never got an interview simply because they did not think properly about their UCAS application; they relied on their hope that the selectors would somehow see through the words and get an instinctive feeling about them.

The following sections will tell you more about what the selectors are looking for, and how you can avoid common mistakes. Before looking at how the selectors go about deciding whom to call to interview, there are a number of important things that you need to think about.

The principal importance is your personal statement, as this is your chance to show the university selectors three very important themes. These are:

1| why you want to be a doctor
2| what you have done to investigate the profession
3| whether you are the right sort of person for their medical school (in other words, the personal qualities that make you an outstanding candidate).

Thus the personal statement is your opportunity to demonstrate to the selectors that you not only have researched medicine thoroughly, but that you also have the right personal qualities to succeed as a doctor. Do not be tempted to write the statement in the sort of formal English that you find in, for example, job applications. Read through a draft of your statement and ask yourself the question 'Does it sound like me?' If not, rewrite it. Avoid phrases such as 'I was fortunate enough to be able to shadow a doctor' when you really just mean 'I shadowed a doctor' or 'I arranged to shadow a doctor'.

Why medicine?

Your personal statement must, fundamentally, convince admissions tutors of your interest in following a career in medicine.

A high proportion of UCAS applications contain a sentence like 'From an early age I have wanted to be a doctor because it is the only career that combines my love of science with the chance to work with people.' Admissions tutors not only get bored with reading this, but it is also clearly untrue: if you think about it, there are many careers that combine science and people, including teaching, pharmacy, physiotherapy and nursing. However, the basic ideas behind this sentence may well apply to you. If so, you need to personalise it. You could mention an incident that first got you interested in medicine – a visit to your own doctor, a conversation with a family friend, or a lecture at school, for instance. You could write about your interest in human biology or a biology project that you undertook when you were younger to illustrate your interest in science, and you could give examples of how you like to work with others. The important thing is to back up your initial interest with your efforts to investigate the career.

A sample statement can be found below. It is an excellent personal statement made by a mature student. Don't be put off by the sophistication and/or achievements of this student, but understand that a lot of thinking and time went into this statement. You also have your style and achievements, and what you have to do is write the statement in such a manner that captures the reader's imagination and leaves them under no illusion that you are primarily focused on medicine as a vocation for life. Here, the example demonstrates clarity and focus, and what comes through the most is the enthusiasm that the candidate has for medicine. These attributes will give the applicant an excellent chance of being called in for an interview and/or just being given an offer.

To say I have always wanted to be a doctor would be untrue. But I have always wanted a career that motivates me to work hard, challenges my intellect and rewards my sense of responsibility, both to individuals and the wider community.

As an undergraduate at Harvard University, I majored in Psychology before switching to History of Art; I went on to intern at an art museum and Sotheby's auction house for two summers. After graduating I became an assistant editor at Viking Penguin in New York, which spurred my decision to return to academia for a Master's degree in literature at UCL.

Whilst studying for my MA, I reconnected with an old interest: medicine. As a teenager I volunteered at a rehabilitation hospital and loved my rounds in the paediatric ward, speaking to patients and families and having an impact on their healthcare experiences.

As a psychology undergraduate, I was thrilled by the academic rigour of the research being done in the bone density and endocrinology laboratory where I worked for a summer. I found the mechanisms of the pharmaceuticals they were studying fascinating as well as the way in which data was collected and processed and in turn led to quantifiable results and further medical progress. So when I became a fundraiser and academic event planner at the Royal Society of Medicine, it was with a sense of familiarity that I re-entered the medical world. Over the past year and a half, I have coordinated meetings where high-level subjects, such as the role of prions in Alzheimer's disease, are being discussed, and I have been unfailingly intrigued by the topics and eager to learn more. The longer I worked at the RSM and the more I spoke to different doctors, the more certain I became that medicine was the right profession for me.

To broaden my medical experiences within a hospital environment, I began volunteering at UCLH in the evenings, bringing food to patients, helping them eat and discussing everything from the weather to World War II to cricket. My nights at UCLH reinforced for me the incredible individuality of patients and that no two people, despite having the same diagnosis, will ever have exactly the same experience of a disease. This message was recently reiterated whilst shadowing in the radiology department at Kent and Sussex hospital; I am now fascinated by the various uses of imaging in medicine, from CT scans to identify malignant tumours to cardiac catheters for angiograms – I was even lucky enough to watch the intricate and exciting process of inserting stents – but I also observed the vitally important interactions between patient and doctor. I could not help but notice how much of a doctor's day is spent listening to patients and communicating with them about their disease or condition and how essential this exchange of information is to achieving the best possible treatment.

Through my experiences at the RSM, UCLH and shadowing, I have realised that medicine is the career I have been looking for: it is a force for good, with direct impact on people's lives, a constantly changing (and therefore challenging) field. It is not a career carried out in intellectual isolation or done solely for financial gain. Medicine is dynamic, thought provoking and interpersonal, and for all these reasons I want to be a part of it. Over the next year I will be doing work experience in medical microbiology and pulmonology, whilst continuing my rounds at UCLH; with these experiences to come, I head back to school to complete the requisite A levels secure in the knowledge that I am investing in an exciting and well-researched future.

So to say that I've always wanted to be a doctor would be untrue. But now, I absolutely do.

WARNING!

Do not write any of the above passages in your personal statement, as admissions tutors are all too aware of the existence of this book. Ensure that your personal statement answer is not only personal to you, but also honest.

Timing

The UCAS submission period is from 1 September to 15 January, but medical applications have to be with UCAS by 15 October. Late applications are also permitted, although medical schools are not bound to consider them. Remember that most referees take at least a week to consult the relevant teachers and compile a reference, so allow for that and aim to submit your application by 1 September unless there is a good reason for delaying.

The only convincing reason for delaying is that your teachers cannot predict high A level grades at the moment, but might be able to do so if they see high-quality work during the autumn term. If you are not on track for AAB/ABB by October, you still need to submit your application because, without an entry in the UCAS system, you cannot participate in Clearing.

TIP!

Keep a copy of your personal statement so that you can look at it when you prepare for the interview.

What happens next and what to do about it

Once your reference has been submitted, a receipt will be sent to your school or college to acknowledge its arrival. Your application is then processed and UCAS will send you confirmation of your details. If you don't receive this, you should check with your referee that it has been correctly submitted. The confirmation will contain your application number, your details and the list of courses you have applied to. Check carefully to make sure that the details in your application have been saved to the UCAS system correctly. At the same time, make a note of your UCAS number – you will need to quote this when you contact the medical schools.

Now comes a period of waiting, which can be very unsettling but which must not distract you from your studies. Most medical schools decide whether or not they want to interview you within a month, but there are some categories, such as retake students, who will not be called for interview until the new year; in some cases, the medical school may wait until March, when the results of any January retake exams are known.

If you have applied to one of those medical schools that do not interview A level candidates, the next communication you receive may be a notification from UCAS that you have been made a conditional offer.

If one or more of the medical schools decides to interview you, your next letter will be an invitation to visit the school and attend an interview. (For advice on how to prepare for the interview, see Chapter 3.)

If you are unlucky, the next correspondence you get from UCAS will contain the news that you have been rejected by one or more of your choices. Does that mean it's time to relax on the A level work and dust off alternative plans? Should you be reading up on exactly what the four-year course in 'Road Resurfacing' involves? No, you should not!

A rejection is a setback and it does make the path into medicine that bit steeper, but it isn't an excuse to give up. A rejection should act as a spur to work even harder because the grades you achieve at A level are now even more important. Don't give up and do turn to page 60 to see what to do when you get your A level results.

Answer to BMAT sample question on page 21: **C**

03 Getting an offer

The idea of preparing for an interview is a relatively new one, and there are still many people who feel that you can't (or shouldn't) do so. Nevertheless, there is a fundamental weakness in the theory that the panel will somehow dismiss what you say and how you look as they unerringly uncover the 'real you'. Wise and experienced though the interviewers may be, they do not have the ability to examine the deep recesses of the soul. They cannot ignore the words you didn't mean to say or supply the ones you left out.

■ Making your interview a success

Success in an interview, like success in any other human activity, depends on preparation and practice. The first time you try to do something, you usually get it wrong, if only because unfamiliarity leads to nervousness. Practice is particularly important because medical schools rarely give a second chance to someone who makes a bad impression at interview.

To help you practise, this chapter lists many typical questions and includes discussion on how to answer them. There is a section on how you can take charge of the interview and encourage the interviewers to ask you the questions you want to answer. There is a list of sample questions for a mock interview and, finally, there is a brief explanation of what will happen after your interviews.

The questions included here are real questions that have been put to applicants over the last two years. They have been gleaned from students who have faced interviews, from admissions tutors and through sitting in on the real thing. As explained later, you cannot prepare for the odd, unpredictable questions, but the interviewers are not trying to catch you out, and they can be relied on to ask some of the general questions that are discussed here.

For many questions, there are no 'right' answers and, even if there were, you shouldn't trot them out parrot fashion. The purpose of presenting the questions, and some strategies for answering them, is to help you think about your answers before the interview and to enable you to put forward your own views clearly and with confidence.

When you have read through this section, and thought about the questions, arrange for someone to sit down with you and take you through the mock interview questions. (If you have the facilities, you will find it helpful to record the interview on video, for later analysis.) You might be interested in the views of four medical professionals, quoted in the November 2002 edition of the *Student BMJ*, on the qualities that they look for. This views will not have changed and in fact are time and time again emphasised by professionals in this field.

> *'An understanding about what being a good doctor entails from both the profession's point of view and the patient's point of view; a significant, meaningful experience of working in a healthcare environment or with disabled or disadvantaged people; an understanding of the importance of research in medicine; an awareness of the ethical issues associated with medical research; good oral communication skills and evidence of flexible and critical thinking.'*

Peter McCrorie, Director of the Graduate Entry Programme at St George's

> *'The innate characteristics of a good doctor are beneficence and the capacity to engage with the knowledge necessary for informed practice.'*

Dr Allan Cumming, Associate Dean of Teaching at Edinburgh University

> *'I think that you are born with some personal qualities, such as the ability to get on with people, to empathise with their distress, to inspire confidence in others, and to carry anxiety. Such qualities are very difficult to train into a person. A good doctor also needs knowledge and the experience of implementing that knowledge.'*

Mike Shooter, President of the Royal College of Psychiatrists

> *'A medical student needs to be bright – not least to cope with a lifetime of assimilation of new concepts and knowledge. The ability to communicate, the ability to work as part of a multi-professional team, empathy and a non-prejudicial approach are qualities that should be expected in all healthcare professionals. There is also, however, a need for diversity and a need to resist any move towards personality conformity.'*

John Tooke, Dean of the Peninsula Medical School

Finally, don't forget that medical school interviewers are busy people and they do not interview for the fun of it. Neither do they set out to humiliate you. They call you for interview because they want to offer you a place – make it easy for them to do so!

◼ Typical interview questions and how to handle them

Why do you want to become a doctor?

The question that most interviewees dread! Answers that will turn your interviewers' stomachs and may lead to rejection are:

- ◼ I want to heal sick people
- ◼ my father is a doctor and I want to be like him
- ◼ the money's good and unemployment among doctors is low
- ◼ the careers teacher told me to apply
- ◼ it's glamorous
- ◼ I want to join a respected profession, so it is either this or law.

Try the question now. Most sixth-formers find it quite hard to give an answer and are often not sure why they want to be a doctor. Often the reasons are lost in the mists of time and have simply been reinforced over the years.

The interviewers will be sympathetic, but they do require an answer that sounds convincing. There are four general strategies:

The story (option A)
You tell the interesting (and true) story of how you have always been interested in medicine, how you have made an effort to find out what is involved by visiting your local hospital, working with your GP, etc. and how this long-term and deep-seated interest has now become something of a passion. (Stand by for searching questions designed to check that you know what you are talking about!)

The story (option B)
You tell the interesting (and true) story of how you, or a close relative, suffered from an illness that brought you into contact with the medical profession. This experience made you think of becoming a doctor and, since then, you have made an effort to find out what is involved ... (as before).

The logical elimination of alternatives
In this approach you have analysed your career options and decided that you want to spend your life in a scientific environment (you have enjoyed science at school) but would find pure research too impersonal. Therefore the idea of a career that combines the excitement of scientific investigation with a great deal of human contact is attractive. Since discovering that medicine offers this combination, you have investigated it (and other alternatives) thoroughly (visits to hospitals, GPs, etc.) and have become passionately committed to your decision.

The problems with this approach are that:

- ◼ they will have heard it all before
- ◼ you will find it harder to convince them of your passion for medicine.

Fascination with people

Some applicants can honestly claim to have a real interest in people. Here's a test to see if you are one of them: you are waiting in the queue for a bus/train/supermarket checkout. Do you ignore the other people in the queue or do you start chatting to them? Win extra points if they spontaneously start chatting to you, and a bonus if, within five minutes, they have told you their life story. Applicants with this seemingly magical power to empathise with their fellow human beings do, if they have a matching interest in human biology, have a good claim to a place at medical school.

Whether you choose one of these strategies or one of your own, your answer must be well considered and convincing. Additionally, it should sound natural and not over-rehearsed. Bear in mind that most of your interviewers will be doctors, and they (hopefully) will have chosen medicine because they, like you, had a burning desire to do so. They will not expect you to be able to justify your choice by reasoned argument alone. Statements (as long as they are supported by evidence of practical research) such as 'and the more work I did at St James's, the more I realised that medicine is what I desperately want to do' are quite acceptable and far more convincing than saying 'Medicine is the only career that combines science and the chance to work with people', because it isn't!

> 'We make allowances for the fact that students are going to be nervous at the interview. Indeed, if the applicant is not at all nervous I would question their desire to become a doctor. We try to relax students at the beginning by asking them questions that they are expecting, for example, why medicine? We know that this is a question that students worry about, but we also know that they have probably prepared an answer for this. After this, we ask about work experience or voluntary work because this is when we can see whether they are really serious. What we are after is evidence that the student was interested in what was going on around them, and that they gained something from the experience. It is not difficult to arrange voluntary work in some capacity, so it is what they got out of it which is important, not simply having done it.'

Admissions Tutor

What have you done to show your commitment to medicine and to the community?

This should tie in with your UCAS application. Your answer should demonstrate that you do have a genuine interest in helping others. Ideally, you will have a track record of regular visits to your local hospital or hospice, where you will have worked in the less attractive side of patient care (such as cleaning bedpans). Acceptable alternatives are regular visits to an elderly person to do their chores, or work with one of the charities that care for the homeless or other disadvantaged groups.

It isn't sufficient to have worked in a laboratory, out of sight of patients, or to have done so little work as to be trivial: 'I once walked around the ward of the local hospital – it was very nice.' You may find that an answer such as this leads the interviewer to ask: 'If you enjoyed working in the hospital so much, why don't you want to become a nurse?' This is a tough question. You need to indicate that, while you admire enormously the work that nurses do, you would like the challenge of diagnosis and of deciding what treatment should be given.

You also need to ask yourself why admissions tutors ask about work experience. Is it because they want you to demonstrate your commitment, or because they want to know whether you have stamina, a caring nature, communication skills and, above all, the interest necessary for a medical career? If it was simply a matter of ticking boxes, then they probably would not bother to ask you about it at the interview. They ask you questions because they want to know whether you were there in body only, or if you were genuinely engaged with what was happening around you.

Why have you applied to this medical school?

Don't say:

- it's well equipped
- I like the buildings
- it's easy to get into
- my dad's the Dean
- it has a good reputation (that is, unless you know exactly what for).

Some of the reasons that you might have are given below.

- **Thorough investigation.** You have made a thorough investigation of a number of the medical schools that you have considered. You have been to an open day and have talked to current medical students. You have spoken to the admissions tutor about your particular situation and asked their advice about suitable work experience, and he or she was particularly encouraging and helpful. You feel that the general atmosphere is one you would love to be part of.
- **Course structure.** You have read the prospectus (don't forget to) and feel that the course is structured in an interesting way. You like the fact that it is integrated and that students are brought into contact with patients at an early date. Another related reason might be that you are attracted by the subject-based or systems-based teaching approach.
- **Recommendation from teacher.** Your careers teacher at school recommended the school. Careers teachers make it their business to find out about individual medical schools, and they will also receive feedback from their former pupils. An informed recommendation is a

perfectly valid reason for choosing a particular medical school. The same applies to advice you may read in this or other books.

■ **Recommendation from friend.** A variation on the careers teacher theme: you may have a recommendation from your friends or informed friends of your parents. In this case, you must be able to quote the names of these friends.

Don't forget that all UK medical schools and university departments of medicine are well equipped and offer a high standard of teaching. It is therefore perfectly reasonable to say that, while you have no specific preference at this stage, you do have a great deal to give to any school that offers you a place. This answer will inevitably lead on to: 'Well, tell us what you do have to give.' That question is discussed on page 50.

> 'We give the interviewees a questionnaire to fill in before they have their interviews. We do this because it creates more time in the interview to ask them more about themselves. Although the questionnaire is important, it is not as important as a good, confident performance in the interview itself. I want the applicants to realise that if they perform well in the interview, the questionnaire is not going to adversely affect my decision as long as it is written in reasonably good English. Conversely, a brilliantly written questionnaire is not going to get a student a place if he or she performs badly at the interview.'

Admissions Tutor

Questions designed to assess your knowledge of medicine

No one expects you to know all about your future career before you start at medical school, but they do expect you to have made an effort to find out something about it. If you are really interested in medicine, you will have a reasonable idea of common illnesses and diseases, and you will be aware of topical issues. The questions aimed at testing your knowledge of medicine divide into seven main areas:

1| the human body (and what can go wrong with it)
2| Discussing major medical issues
3| the medical profession
4| the National Health Service: funding health
5| private medicine
6| ethical questions
7| other issues.

The human body (and what can go wrong with it)
The interviewers will expect you to be interested in medicine and to be aware of current problems and new treatments. In both cases the list is endless, but the following are some areas with which you should familiarise yourself.

Your area of interest. This is how the questions might go.

> **Interviewer:** You have written on your UCAS application that you are interested in how the human body works. Which system particularly interests you?
>
> **Candidate:** Um, the brain.
>
> **Interviewer:** Tell us how the brain works.
>
> **Candidate:** Um, oh dear. I'm very sorry, I've forgotten.
>
> **Interviewer:** (with pleasure as they spring the trap) Well, that's a real pity because there are only two people in the world who know how the brain works. One is God and he won't tell us and the other is you and you've forgotten. (Laughs all round at your expense.)

Avoid this trap by choosing, in advance, a relatively well-understood body system, e.g. the cardiovascular system, then learn how it works and (particularly for interviews at Oxbridge) prepare for fundamental questions such as 'What is meant by myocardial infarction?' and questions about what can go wrong with the system – see below.

Your work experience. If you are able to arrange work experience in a medical environment, you will want to include it in your personal statement, but make sure that you keep a diary and that you enter in it not only what you saw, but also medical details of what was happening.

For example, note not only that a patient was brought into casualty but what the symptoms were, what the diagnosis was and what treatment was given. Here is an example of a bad answer.

> **Interviewer:** I notice that you spent two weeks at St James's. Tell me something about what you did there.
>
> **Candidate:** I spent two days in the Cardiology department, three days in A&E, one day in the Pathology lab, two days on an Oncology ward, one and a half days in Neurology and half a day in General Surgical. I saw sutures, drips, lung cancer … [etc.].

The problem here is that the interviewers are no clearer about your suitability for a career in medicine, only that you have a good memory. This approach is referred to by some admissions tutors as medical tourism. Interviewers are looking for a genuine enthusiasm for medicine. They are not going to be impressed by a long list of hospital departments, treatments or illnesses unless they can see that your experience actually meant something to you on a personal level, and that you gained insights into the profession. Here is a better answer:

'I was able to spend time in a number of wards, which enabled me to see a whole range of treatments. For instance, during my two

days in the Cardiology department, I was able to see several newly admitted patients who might have had heart attacks. I found it particularly interesting to see how careful the doctors had to be in taking the history, so that they were not putting words into the patients' mouths about their symptoms and the type of pain they were experiencing. I was also able to watch an angioplasty being performed. I was amazed at the level of skill the surgeon demonstrated – I would love to do that myself one day.'

In this type of answer, your genuine enthusiasm, good observation and respect for the profession are all apparent.

'One piece of advice I would give any potential interviewee is to try to guess what we, the interviewers, might be worried about in their application, and try to address this in the interview. For example, the student who had not done much voluntary work at time the UCAS form had been submitted but who had done more since should mention this. There are many ways to do this, perhaps by responding to a question about why they want to be a doctor by saying "... and the recent work experience I have done at X demonstrated ...". Another example is if a student has not written much about extracurricular activities, possibly because the school does not offer much or because the student has a part-time job. This could be brought into the conversation when responding to questions about how he or she copes with stress, or about communication skills. The interviewee needs to realise that if weak areas are not covered in the interview, then we will probably be as concerned after the interview as we were before.'

Admissions Tutor

Discussing major medical issues

Keeping a file of cuttings

Make sure that you read *New Scientist, Student BMJ* and, on a daily basis, a broadsheet newspaper that carries regular, high-quality medical reporting. The *Independent* has excellent coverage of current health issues, and the *Guardian*'s health section on Tuesdays is informative and interesting. Newspapers' websites often group articles thematically, which can save time. The Sunday broadsheets often contain comprehensive summaries of the week's top medical stories.

The big killers

Diseases affecting the circulation of the blood (including heart disease) and cancer are the main causes of death in the UK. Make sure you know the factors that contribute towards them and the strategies for prevention and treatment. You can read more about this in Chapter 8, 'Current issues'.

The global picture

You may well be asked about what is happening on a global scale. You should know about the biggest killers (infectious diseases and circulatory diseases), trends in population changes, the role of the World Health Organization (WHO), and the differences in medical treatments between developed and developing countries. You can read more about this in the 'Current issues' chapter.

The Human Genome Project and gene therapy

You would be wise to familiarise yourself with the sequence of developments in the field of genetic research, starting with the discovery of the double helix structure of DNA by Crick and Watson in 1953. You should find out all that you can about:

- recombinant DNA technology (gene therapy, genetic engineering)
- genetic diagnosis (of particular interest to insurance companies)
- cloning (see page 114)
- stem cell research
- GM crops
- genetic enhancement of livestock
- 'pharming'.

Fashionable illnesses

At any one time, the media tend to concentrate on one or two 'fashionable' diseases. The papers fill their pages with news of the latest 'epidemic' and the general public is expected to react as if the great plague of 1665 were just round the corner. In reality, Ebola, CJD and SARS resulted in very small numbers of deaths, and the same can be said of swine flu, for example. The media encourage us to react emotionally rather than logically in matters concerning risk. They advise us to stop eating beef but not to stop driving our cars, even though around 3,000 people are killed in road accidents every year. Thus, it is good to be aware of this bias as universities at interviews may ask you why it is that despite higher death rates due to obesity or alcoholism, swine flu is getting 'all the attention'.

While these diseases tend to be trivial in terms of their effect, they are often interesting in scientific terms, and the fact that they are being discussed in the media makes it likely that they will come up at interview.

A typical question would be: 'Why is swine flu causing so much concern, when very few people have died from it?' It is important to know something about these illnesses (see Chapter 8 and www.mpw.co.uk/getintomed for links to information on bird flu, SARS, MRSA, mad cows and CJD) but equally important to keep them in statistical proportion. For example, nearly 2 million people die as a result of contracting diarrhoeal infections each year, mostly the result of poor sanitation and infected water supplies, and over 5 million people die as a result of injury sustained in accidents or violence.

Diet, exercise and the environment

The maintenance of health on a national scale isn't simply a matter of waiting until people get ill and then rushing in with surgery or medicine to cure them. There is good evidence that illness can be prevented by a sensible diet, not smoking, taking exercise and living in a healthy environment. In this context, a healthy environment means one where food and water are uncontaminated by bacteria and living quarters are well ventilated, warm and dry. The huge advance in health and life expectancy since the middle of the nineteenth century owes much more to these factors than to the achievements of modern medicine.

TIP!

When discussing medical topics, you will sound more convincing if you learn and use the correct terminology. For example, to a doctor, a patient doesn't turn up at the surgery with high blood pressure; they present with hypertension. The best sources of correct terminology are medical textbooks, some of which are quite easy to understand (see Chapter 9).

The medical profession

The typical question is: 'What makes a good doctor?' Avoid answering: 'A caring and sympathetic nature.' If these really were the crucial qualities of a good doctor, there would be little point in going to medical school. Start by stressing the importance of the aspects that can be taught and, in particular, emphasise the technical qualities that a doctor needs: the ability to carry out a thorough examination, to diagnose accurately and quickly what is wrong and the skill to choose and organise the correct treatment.

After this comes the ability to communicate effectively and sympathetically with the patient so that he or she can understand and participate in the treatment. The most important part of communication is listening. There is an old medical adage that if you listen to the patient for long enough he or she will give you the diagnosis.

Communication skills also have an important role to play in treatment – studies have shown that some patients get better more quickly when they feel involved and as part of the medical team. The best way to answer a question about what qualities are necessary to be a successful doctor is to refer to your work experience. You could say: 'The ability to react quickly. For example, when I was shadowing Dr Ferguson at the Fletcher Memorial Hospital, I witnessed a case where ...'.

The National Health Service: funding health

An application to a medical school is also an application for a job, and you should have taken the trouble to find out something about your likely future employer. You should be aware of the structure of the NHS and the role that Strategic Health Authorities, Primary Care Trusts and Foundation Hospitals play. You need to know about the recent changes in the way that doctors are trained, and the career paths that are open to medical graduates. When you are doing your work experience, you should take every opportunity to discuss the problems in the NHS with the doctors that you meet. They will be able to give you first-hand accounts of what is happening, and this is a very effective way of coping with questions on the NHS.

A typical interview question is: 'What are the main problems facing the NHS?' The most impressive way to answer this is to say something along the lines of: 'Well, when I was shadowing Dr Jones at St James's Hospital, we discussed this. In his opinion, they are ...'. This not only demonstrates that you were using your work experience to increase your awareness of the medical profession, but it also takes the pressure off you because you are not having to come up with your own views. However, be prepared to then discuss your answer in more depth.

Private medicine

Another set of questions that needs careful thought concerns private medicine. Don't forget that many consultants have flourishing private practices and rely on private work for a major part of their income. Equally, a number of doctors do not have the opportunity to practise privately and may resent a system that allows some consultants to earn money both within and outside the NHS.

Your best bet is to look at the philosophy behind private medicine, and you may care to argue as follows below.

Most people agree that if you are run over by a bus you should be taken to hospital and treated at the taxpayers' expense. In general, urgent treatment for serious and life-threatening conditions should be treated by the NHS and we should all chip in to pay for it. On the other hand, most of us would agree that someone who doesn't particularly care for the shape of their nose and who wants to change it by expensive plastic surgery should pay for the operation themselves. We can't ban cosmetic operations, so we are led to accept the right of private medicine to exist.

Having established these two extremes, one is left to argue about the point where the two systems meet. Should there be a firm dividing line or a fuzzy one where both the NHS and private medicine operate?

You could also point out that private medicine should not harm the NHS. For example, the NHS has a problem of waiting lists. If 10 people are standing in a queue for a bus, everyone benefits if four of those waiting jump into a taxi – providing, of course, that they don't persuade the bus driver to drive it!

TIP!

This example illustrates an effective general technique for answering difficult moral, ethical or legal questions. The interviewers are not particularly interested in your opinion, but they are interested in whether you have understood the issues. Always demonstrate this by explaining the extreme opposing views. Only then, and in a balanced and reasonable way, give your own opinion.

Ethical questions

Medical ethics is a fascinating area of moral philosophy. You won't be expected to answer questions on the finer points but you could be asked about the issues raised below.

A patient who refuses treatment

You could be presented with a scenario, and asked what you would do in the situation. For example, you have to inform a patient that he has cancer. Without radiotherapy and chemotherapy his life expectancy is likely to be a matter of months. The patient tells you that he or she does not wish to be treated. What would you do if you were in this situation? The first thing to remember is that the interviewer is not asking you this question because he or she wants to know what the answer to this problem is. Questions of this nature are designed to see whether you can look at problems from different angles, weigh up arguments, use your knowledge of medical issues to come to a conclusion, and produce coherent and structured answers.

A useful technique for answering 'What would you do if you were a doctor and ...' questions is to start by discussing the information that you would need, or the questions that you might ask the patient. In the above example, you would ask:

- how old is the patient?
- does the patient have any other medical conditions that might affect his life expectancy?
- why is the patient refusing the treatment?

The answer to these questions would then determine what you would do next. The patient could be refusing treatment for religious or moral reasons; it might simply be that he has heard stories about the side effects of the treatment you have recommended. One possible route would be to give him contact details of a suitable support group, counselling service or information centre.

A classic case is someone who refuses a life-saving blood transfusion because it contravenes his or her religious beliefs. Fair enough, you may feel, but what if, on these grounds, a parent refuses to allow a baby's life to be saved by a transfusion? Similarly, in a well-publicised legal case, a woman refused to allow a caesarean delivery of her baby. The judge ruled that the wishes of the mother could be overruled. It is worth noting that the NHS (as a representative of the state) has no right to keep a patient in hospital against his or her will unless the medical team and relatives use the powers of the Mental Health Act.

TIP!

You should remember that the interviewers are not interested in your opinions, but they are interested in whether you have understood the issues. A useful approach to this type of question is:

- explain the background to the question(s)
- consider both sides of the argument
- bring current issues or examples into your answer
- only express a personal opinion at the very end.

Euthanasia

To answer questions on euthanasia, start by making sure that you know the following correct terminology, and the law.

- **Suicide.** The act of killing oneself intentionally.
- **Physician-assisted suicide.** This involves a doctor intentionally giving a person advice on or the means to commit suicide. It describes situations where competent people want to kill themselves but lack either the means or the ability.
- **Euthanasia.** Euthanasia is a deliberate act of omission whose primary intention is to end another's life. Literally, it means a gentle or easy death, but it has come to signify a deliberate intervention with the intention to kill someone, often described as the 'mercy killing' of people in pain with terminal illnesses.
- **Double effect.** The principle of double effect provides the justification for the provision of medical treatment that has a negative effect, although the intention is to provide an overall positive effect. The principle permits an act that foreseeably has both good and bad effects, provided that the good effect is the reason for acting and is not caused by the bad. A common example is the provision of essential pain-relieving drugs in terminal care, at the risk of shortening life. Pain relief is the intention and outweighs the risks of shortening life.
- **Non-treatment.** Competent adults have the right to refuse any treatment, including life-prolonging procedures. The British Medical Association (BMA) does not consider valid treatment refusal by a patient to be suicide. Respecting a competent, informed patient's treatment refusal is not assisting suicide.
- **Withdrawing/withholding life-prolonging medical treatment.** Not all treatment with the potential to prolong life has to be provided in

all circumstances, especially if its effect is seen as extending the dying process. Cardio-pulmonary resuscitation of a terminally ill cancer patient is an extreme example. In deciding which treatment should be offered, the expectation must be that the advantages outweigh the drawbacks for the individual patient.

Currently in the UK there is a ban on assisted suicide. This is a most contentious issue and, as you can imagine, even within the medical community opinion is well divided. In short, it deliberates and questions the ethical conundrum of the right of the individual to 'die with dignity' when they so wish versus those that argue that it goes against moral and religious teaching and that it is against God's law to take a life. The nature of this ethical dilemma is central to the role of a doctor, as some would argue further that it also goes against the moral duty of a doctor, which is to prolong life instead of shortening it. As it is a controversial theme, it is one that can often be asked at interviews. What must be remembered is that aside from your own beliefs, whether you do or don't support euthanasia, the de facto position in the UK is that assisted suicides are currently illegal. There is, however, a Swiss-based group, Dignitas, which to date has helped over 100 residents of Britain to commit suicide. This has been due to their extreme suffering, which has to be well proven and documented. Dignitas was organised in 1998 to help people with chronic diseases to die, honouring the wishes of the patient and those around them to end their suffering. There is currently nothing stopping UK nationals from travelling to Switzerland and being assisted to commit suicide, but as the law stands loved ones and friends may be prosecuted if they help. See Euthanasia and Assisted deaths in Chapter 8.

So one of the key questions is: 'Could you withdraw treatment from a patient for whom the prognosis was very poor, who seemed to enjoy no quality of life and who was in great pain?' The answer to this question comes in two parts. In part one, you must recognise that a decision like this could not be taken without the benefit of full medical training and some experience, together with the advice of colleagues and the fullest consultation with the patient and his or her relations, as well as knowing your position according to the law. If, after that process, it was clear that life support should be withdrawn, then, and only then, would you take your decision. Part two involves convincing the panel that, having taken your decision, you would act on it.

Other issues

A good opening question is: 'Should smokers be treated on the NHS?' On the one hand, it is certainly true that smoking is a contributory factor in heart disease. Is it fair to expect the community as a whole to spend a great deal of money on, for example, coronary artery bypass surgery if the patient refuses to abandon behaviour that could jeopardise the long-term effectiveness of the operation? Conversely, one can argue that all citizens and certainly all taxpayers have the right to treatment irrespective of their lifestyles. Further to this, one can argue that duty paid on cigarettes adds up to more than the cost of treatment.

Another series of questions recognises the fact that there is a limit to the resources available to the NHS and highlights the tough decisions that may need to be taken. The interviewer might refer to 'rationing of healthcare'. Suppose you have resources for one operation but two critically ill patients – how do you decide which one to save? Or, suppose that you can perform six hip replacement operations for the cost of one coronary artery bypass. Heart bypass operations save life; hip replacements merely improve it. Which option should you go for?

Even more controversial issues surround surgery to change gender. Should these operations be performed when the money could be used to save, or at least prolong, life?

Events are constantly bringing fresh moral issues associated with medicine into the public arena. It is important that you read the papers and maintain an awareness of the current 'hot' issues. See Chapter 9 for further reading.

Questions aimed at finding out whether you will fit in

One of the reasons for interviewing you is to see whether you will fit successfully into both the medical school and the medical profession. The interviewers will try to find out if your views and approach to life are likely to make you an acceptable colleague in a profession that, to a great extent, depends on teamwork. This does not mean that they want to hear views identical to their own. On the contrary; they will welcome ideas that are refreshing and interesting. What they do not like to hear is arrogance, lies, bigotry or tabloid headlines.

These questions have another important purpose: to assess your ability to communicate in a friendly and effective way with strangers even when under pressure. This skill will be very important when you come to deal with patients.

Questions about your UCAS application

The personal statement section, in which you write about yourself, is a fertile area for questions; as explained earlier, you should have included some juicy morsels to attract the interviewers. The most successful interviews often revolve around some interesting or amusing topic that is fun to talk about and that makes you stand out from the crowd. The trouble is that you cannot invent such a topic – it really has to exist. Nevertheless, if you really have been involved in a campaign to save an obscure species of toad and can tell a couple of amusing stories about it (make them short), so much the better.

Even if your UCAS application seems, in retrospect, a bit dull, don't worry. Work out something interesting to say. Look at what you wrote and at all costs avoid the really major disasters; if you put that you like reading, for instance, make sure you can remember and talk intelligently about the last book you read.

Sometimes an amusing comment on your application followed up by a relaxed and articulate performance at the interview will do the trick. A good example is the comment that a student made about lasting only three days as a waitress during the summer holidays. She was able to tell a story about dropped food and dry-cleaning bills, and was offered a place. Of course, failing at a part-time job is only going to be a funny story if you are relaxed enough to make it amusing; by then you will have already proved to the interviewers that you are a strong candidate, for whom this incident was an anomaly.

Questions about your contribution to the life of the medical school

These questions can come in many forms but, once identified, they need to be tackled carefully. If you say you like social life, the selectors might worry that you won't pass your pre-clinical exams. On the other hand, if you say that you plan to spend all your time windsurfing, mountaineering or fishing, they'll see you as a loner.

The best approach is probably to say that you realise that medical school is hard work and that your main responsibility must be to pass your exams. After that, you could say that the medical school can only function as a community if the individuals involved are prepared to participate enthusiastically in as many of the extracurricular activities as possible. Above all, try to talk about communal and team activities rather than more solitary pursuits.

You may find it helpful to know that, in one London medical school, the interviewers are told to ask themselves if the candidate has made good use of the opportunities available to them, and whether they have the personal qualities and interests appropriate to student life and a subsequent career in medicine. Poor communication skills, excessive shyness or lack of enthusiasm concern them, and will be taken into account when awarding scores.

Unpredictable questions

There are two types of unpredictable question: the nice and the nasty.

Nice questions

Nice questions are usually designed to test your communication skills and to assess your personality. A typical nice question would be: '*If you won a million pounds on the lottery, what would you do with it?*'

- Rule 1. Don't relax! Your answer to this question needs to be as effective and articulate as any other and, while you should appear to be relaxed, you must not let your thinking or speech become sloppy.
- Rule 2. A nice question could also indicate that the interviewer has decided against you and simply wants to get through the allotted time as easily as possible. If you suspect that this is the case (possibly because you have said something that you now regret), this question provides an opportunity to redeem yourself. Try to steer the questions back to gritty, medical-related topics. See the advice on page 51.

Nasty questions

The 'interview nasties' are included either as a test of your reaction to pressure or in response to something you have said in answer to a previous question. Here are some examples.

- Why should we give you a place here when we have many better qualified applicants?
- Don't you think that someone with the views you have just expressed would find it almost impossible to function effectively as an NHS doctor?

There are no right answers but there is a correct approach. Start by fixing the interviewer with a big smile, then distance the question from your own case. Taking the first question, you could say that you realise that medical school selection is a tough business and that the criteria must be hard to define. On the one hand, it must be tempting to select those whose previous work indicates that they will sail through their pre-clinical exams but, on the other, you can think of brilliant academics who find it hard to communicate. You believe that you do have something to offer the profession.

In general, the technique, once again, is to identify the extreme answers to the question and then, almost as an afterthought, give your own position. This approach shows the interviewers that you are capable of logical reasoning under pressure.

Questions about your own academic performance

These are especially likely if you are retaking A levels (or have retaken them). The question will be: 'Why did you do so badly in your A levels?' Don't say 'I'm thick and lazy', however true you feel that is!

Another bad ploy is to blame your teachers. It is part of the unspoken freemasonry of teaching that no teacher likes to hear another teacher blamed for poor results. If, however, your teacher was absent for part of the course, it is perfectly acceptable to explain this. You should also explain any other external circumstances such as illness or family problems, even if you believe them to have been included in the UCAS reference. Sadly, most applicants don't have one of these cast-iron excuses!

The best answer, if you can put your hand on your heart when you deliver it, is to say that you were so involved in other school activities (head of school, captain of cricket, rowing and athletics, chairman of the Community Action Group and producer of the school play) that your work suffered. You can't really be blamed for getting the balance between work and your other activities a little bit skewed and, even if you don't have a really impressive list of other achievements, you should be able to construct an answer on this basis. You might also add that the setback allowed you to analyse your time-management skills, and that you now feel you are much more effective in your use of time.

You may also be asked how you expect to do in your A level exams. You need to show that you are working hard, enjoying the subjects and expect to achieve at least ABB (or more probably AAB – check Table 8 on pages 134–5 for admissions policies to the different medical schools).

Your questions for the interviewers

At the end of the interview, the person chairing the panel may ask if you have any questions you would like to put to the interviewers. Bear in mind that the interviews are carefully timed, and that your attempts to impress the panel with 'clever' questions may do quite the opposite. The golden rule is: only ask a question if you are genuinely interested in the answer (which, of course, you were unable to find during your careful reading of the prospectus and website). Some medical schools, including Keele, will not allow you to ask questions of the interviewing panel. This is mainly because interviews are carefully timed. Questions at Keele can be asked of other staff or current students during the time you are there, but not actually in the interview itself.

Questions to avoid

- What is the structure of the first year of the course?
- Will I be able to live in a hall of residence?
- When will I first have contact with patients?
- Can you tell me about the intercalated BSc option?

As well as being dull questions, the answers to these will be available in the prospectus and on the website, and you will show that you have obviously not done any serious research.

Questions you could ask

- I haven't studied physics at A level. Do you think I should go through some physics textbooks before the start of the course? (This shows that you are keen, and that you want to make sure that you can cope with the course. It will give them a chance to talk about the extra course they offer for non-physicists.)
- Do you think I should try to get more work experience before the start of the course? (Again, an indication of your keenness.)
- Earlier, I couldn't answer the question you asked me on why smoking causes coronary heart disease. What is the reason? (Something that you genuinely might want to know.)
- How soon will you let me know if I have been successful or not?

End by saying: 'All of my questions have been answered by the prospectus and the students who showed me around the medical school. Thank you very much for an enjoyable day.' Big smile, shake hands and say goodbye.

How to structure the interview to your advantage

Having read this far you may well be asking yourself what to do if none of the questions discussed comes up. Some of them will. Furthermore, once the interviewers have asked one of the prepared questions, you should be able to lead them on to the others. This technique is very simple, and most interviewers are prepared to go along with it because it makes their job easier. All you have to do is insert a 'signpost' at the end of each answer.

Here is an example. At the end of your answer to why you want to be a doctor you could add: 'I realise, of course, that medicine is moving through a period of exciting challenges and advances.' Now stop and give the interviewer an 'over to you – I'm ready for the next question' look. Unless he or she is really trying to throw you off balance, the next question will be: 'What do you know about these advances?' Off you go with your answer, but at the end you tack on: 'Hand in hand with these technical changes have come changes in the administration of the NHS.' With luck, you'll get a question about the NHS that you can answer and end with a 'signpost' to medical ethics.

You can, if you wish, plan the whole interview so that each answer leads to a new question. The last answer can be linked to the first question so as to form a loop. The interviewers have only to ask one of the questions in the loop and you are off on a pre-planned track.

This idea never works perfectly, but it does enable you to maximise the amount of time you spend on prepared ground – time when, with luck, you'll be making a good impression. The disadvantage, of course, in having a set of prepared answers ready is that there is a temptation to pull one out of the hat regardless of what is actually being asked. The question 'Why do you want to be a doctor?' (which you might be expecting) requires a very different answer to the question 'Was there something that started your interest in being a doctor?'

One final piece of advice on interviews: keep your answers relatively short and to the point. Nothing is more depressing than an answer that rambles on. If you get a question you haven't prepared, pause for thought, give them your best shot in a cheerful, positive voice and then be quiet!

■ Mock interview questions

As explained at the beginning of the chapter, interview technique can be improved with practice. You can use this section of the book as a source of mock interview questions. Your interviewer should ask supplementary questions as appropriate.

- Why do you want to be a doctor? (Supplementary: Are you sure you know what is involved?)
- (If one of your parents is a doctor.) Presumably you chose medicine because of your father or mother?
- What will you do if you don't get an offer from any medical schools?
- What evidence is there that you can cope with stress?
- Why have you applied to this medical school?
- What do you know about the course here?
- Have you come along to an open day here?
- What have you done to demonstrate your commitment to the community?
- What makes a good doctor?
- Why do you think you would make a good doctor?
- What did the doctors you have spoken to think about medicine as a career?
- What is the standard of health like in your area?
- Why is the standard of health more varied in London/Scotland/ developing countries?
- Are you interested in medical research?
- What interests you about medicine? (Follow with questions about this area.)
- What do you know about AIDS? Why is it so hard to treat?
- What is the difference between a heart attack and a stroke?
- What is the link between obesity and ill health?
- What are the implications for doctors of an ageing population?
- What problems do the elderly face?
- What treatment can doctors offer to the very old?
- What do you think of homeopathy/acupuncture?

- How does diet affect health?
- How does the environment affect health?
- It was thought that tuberculosis (TB) had been eradicated. Why do you think that the number of TB cases is now on the increase?
- What roles can computers/technology play in medicine?
- Tell me about a recent article on medicine/science that you have read. Explain it.
- What are the main causes of ill health where you live?
- What advances in medicine can we look forward to during the next 10/20/50 years?
- What do you think have been the most significant developments in medicine during the last 20/50/100 years?
- What is the biggest threat to humanity over the next 20/50 years, from a medical viewpoint?
- When was the NHS formed?
- Have the reforms of the NHS been successful?
- Should GPs/Primary Care Groups act as fundholders?
- What do you understand by the term rationing/postcode prescribing?
- Do you think private practice by NHS consultants should be abolished?
- Who is the Secretary of State for Health? What would you do if you had to take over this role?
- Can anyone undertake cloning experiments in this country? What are the arguments for and against the cloning of humans?
- Should the UK follow Holland's example and make euthanasia legal?
- Is it right that the NHS should devote resources to sex-change operations when there are long waiting lists for hip replacements?
- Suppose that you were in charge of deciding which of two critically ill babies should have a life-saving operation. Imagine that there was not enough money to operate on both. How would you decide which baby to save?
- Have you come across any examples of ethical problems associated with medicine?
- What are your main interests? (The interviewer must follow up the answer with searching questions.)
- How do you think you will be able to contribute to the life of the medical school?
- What was the last book you read? Can you sum up the story in one minute?
- What do you do in your spare time?
- What is your favourite subject at A level? What do you like about it?
- What is your least favourite subject at A level? What do you dislike about it?
- (For retake candidates or those with disappointing GCSE results) Why did you do badly in your A levels/GCSEs?
- Have you any questions for us?

Points for the interviewer to assess

- Did the candidate answer in a positive, open and friendly way, maintaining eye contact for most of the time?
- Was the candidate's posture such that you felt that he or she was alert, friendly and enthusiastic?
- Was the candidate's voice pitched correctly; neither too loud nor too soft and without traces of arrogance or complacency?
- Was the candidate free of irritating mannerisms?
- Did the candidate's performance reassure you enough not to terrify you at the prospect that he or she could be your doctor in a few years?

The panel

Most medical schools have so many candidates that they operate several interview panels in parallel. This means that your interview may not be chaired by the Dean, but you will certainly have a senior member of the academic staff chairing the panel. He or she will normally be assisted by two or three others. Usually, there are representatives of the clinical and pre-clinical staff and there may be a medical student on the board too. Sometimes a local GP is invited to join the panel. Details of the format of the interview panels can be found in Table 9 on pages 136–7.

While you can expect the interviewers to be friendly, it is possible that one of them may use an aggressive approach. Don't be put off by this; it is a classic interview technique and will usually be balanced by a supportive member of the panel.

Questionnaires

A number of medical schools have introduced a written component to the interview. Some, such as Nottingham, ask for a form or an essay to be sent to them prior to the interview. Others, such as St George's and King's, give each candidate a written exercise on the day of the interview. Bear in mind that a candidate who performs well in the interview, displays the necessary academic and personal qualities and is genuinely suited to medicine is unlikely to be rejected on the basis of the written element.

Dress, posture and mannerisms

You should dress smartly for your interview, but you should also feel comfortable. You will not be able to relax if you feel over-formal. For men, a jacket with a clean shirt and tie is ideal. Women should avoid big earrings, plunging necklines and short skirts. Men should not wear earrings, white socks or loud ties, or have (visible) piercings. They should avoid unconventional hairstyles: no Mohicans or skinheads.

Your aim must be to give an impression of good personal organisation and cleanliness. Make a particular point of your hair and fingernails – you never see a doctor with dirty fingernails. Always polish your shoes before an interview, as this type of detail will be noticed. Don't go in smelling strongly of garlic, aftershave or perfume. You will be invited to sit down, but don't fall back expansively into an armchair, cross your legs and press your fingertips together in an impersonation of Sherlock Holmes. Sit slightly forward in a way that allows you to be both comfortable and alert. Make sure that you arrive early and are well prepared for the interview.

Try to achieve eye contact with each member of the panel and, as much as possible, address your answer directly to the panel member who asked the question (glancing regularly at the others), not up in the air or to a piece of furniture. Most importantly, try to relax and enjoy the interview. This will help you to project an open, cheerful personality.

Finally, watch out for irritating mannerisms. These are easily checked if you videotape a mock interview. The interviewers will not listen to what you are saying if they are all watching to see when you are next going to scratch your left ear with your right thumb!

■ What happens next?

When you have left the room, the person chairing the interview panel will discuss your performance with the other members and will make a recommendation to the Dean. The recommendation will be one of the following:

- accept
- discuss further/waiting list
- reject.

'Accept' means that you will receive a conditional or unconditional offer, usually the standard one. 'Discuss further' means that you are borderline, and may or may not receive an offer, depending on the quality of the applicants seen by other interview panels. If, having been classified as 'discuss further', you have been unlucky and have received a rejection, the medical school may put you on an official or unofficial waiting list. The people on the waiting list are the first to be considered in Clearing. If you have been rejected by all of the institutions you applied to, you can go through the UCAS Extra scheme, which gives you a chance to approach other universities.

Details can be found on the UCAS website.

'Reject' means that you have not been made an offer. You may be luckier at one of the other medical schools to which you have applied.

The official notification of your fate will come to you from UCAS within a few weeks of the interview. If you have been rejected it is helpful to know whether you are on the waiting list and whether or not there is any point in applying again to that medical school. Understandably, the staff will be reluctant to talk to you about your performance, but most medical schools will discuss your application with your UCAS referee if he or she calls them to ask what advice should now be given to you. It is well worth asking your referee to make that telephone call.

04 Results day

The A level results will arrive at your school on the third Thursday in August. The medical schools will have received them a few days earlier. You must make sure that you are at home on the day the results are published. Don't wait for the school to post the results slip to you. Get the staff to tell you the news as soon as possible. If you need to act to secure a place, you may have to act quickly. This chapter will take you through the steps you should follow – for example you may need to use the Clearing system because you have good grades but no offer. It also explains what to do if your grades are disappointing.

■ What to do if things go wrong during the exams

If something happens when you are preparing for or actually taking the exams that prevents you from doing your best, you must notify both the exam board and the medical schools that have made you offers. This notification will come best from your head teacher and should include your UCAS number. Send it off at once; it is no good waiting for disappointing results and then telling everyone that you felt ghastly at the time but said nothing to anyone. Exam boards can give you special consideration if the appropriate forms are sent to them by the school, along with supporting evidence.

Your extenuating circumstances must be convincing. A 'slight sniffle' won't do! If you really are sufficiently ill to be unable to prepare for the exams or to perform effectively during them, you must consult your GP and obtain a letter describing your condition.

The other main cause of under-performance is distressing events at home. If a member of your immediate family is very seriously ill, you should explain this to your head teacher and ask him or her to write to the examiners and medical schools.

With luck, the exam board will give you the benefit of the doubt if your marks fall on a grade border. Equally, you can hope that the medical school will allow you to slip one grade below the conditional offer. If things work out badly, then the fact that you declared extenuating circumstances should ensure that you are treated sympathetically when you reapply through UCAS.

The medical school admissions departments are well organised and efficient, but they are staffed by human beings. If there were extenuating circumstances that could have affected your exam performance and that were brought to their notice in June, it is a good idea to ask them to review the relevant letters shortly before the exam results are published.

What to do if you hold an offer and get the grades

If you previously received a conditional offer and your grades equal or exceed that offer, congratulations! You can relax and wait for your chosen medical school to send you joining instructions. One word of warning: you cannot assume that grades of AAC satisfy an ABB offer. This is especially true if the C grade is in Chemistry.

What to do if you have good grades but no offer

Every year, UCAS statistics reveal that around 300 people get into medical school through Clearing. However, that does not mean that all of these were students who were not holding offers but who nevertheless gained places – many of them were students who narrowly missed their offers but were given places based on their strong performance at interview or because of extenuating circumstances.

Very few schools keep places open and, of those that do, most will choose to allow applicants who hold a conditional offer to slip a grade rather than dust off a reserve list of those they interviewed but didn't make an offer to. Still less are they likely to consider applicants who appear out of the blue – however high their grades. That said, it is likely that every summer a few medical schools will have enough unfilled places to consider a Clearing-style application.

If you hold three A grades but were rejected when you applied through UCAS, you need to let the medical schools know that you are out there. The best way to do this is by email. Contact details are listed in the UCAS directory. If you live nearby, you can always deliver a letter in person, talk to the office staff and hope that your application will stand out from the rest.

Set out below is sample text for an email. Don't copy it word for word!

Don't forget that your UCAS referee may be able to help you. Try to persuade him or her to ring the admissions officers on your behalf – he or she will find it easier to get through than you will. If your referee is unable/unwilling to ring, then he or she should, at least, email a note in support of your application. It is best if both emails arrive at the medical school at the same time.

If you are applying to a medical school that did not receive your UCAS application, ask your referee to email or fax a copy of the form. In general, it is best to persuade the medical school to invite you to arrange for the UCAS application to be sent.

If, despite your most strenuous efforts, you are unsuccessful, you need to consider applying again (see below). The other alternative is to use the Clearing system to obtain a place on a degree course related to medicine and hope to be accepted on the medical course after you graduate.

To: Miss M. D. Whyte
Subject: Application to study Medicine at Melchester

Dear Miss Whyte
UCAS no. 09-123456-7

I have just received my A level results, which were:

Biology A, Chemistry A, English A.
I also have a B grade in AS Philosophy.

You may remember that I applied to Melchester but was rejected after interview/was rejected without an interview. I am still very keen to study medicine at Melchester and hope that you will consider me for any places that may now be available.

My head teacher supports my application and is emailing you a reference. Should you wish to contact him, his details are:

Mr C. Harrow,
tel: 0123 456 7891,
fax: 0123 456 7892,
email: c.harrow@melchester.sch.uk.

I can be contacted at the above email address and could attend an interview at short notice.

Yours sincerely,
Lucy Johnson

What to do if you hold an offer but miss the grades

The options

If you have only narrowly missed the required grades (this includes the AAC grade case described above), it is important that you and your referee contact the medical school to put your case before you are rejected. Sample text for another email follows below.

To: Miss M. D. Whyte
Subject: Application to study Medicine at Melchester

Dear Miss Whyte
UCAS no. 09-123456-7

I have just received my A level results, which were:

Chemistry A, Biology A, English C.
I also have a B grade in AS Philosophy.

I hold a conditional offer from Melchester of ABB and I realise that my grades may not meet that offer. Nevertheless I am still determined to study medicine and I hope you will be able to find a place for me this year. May I remind you that at the time of the exams I was recovering from glandular fever.

A medical certificate was sent to you in June by my head teacher. My head teacher supports my application and is emailing you a reference. Should you wish to contact him, his details are:

Mr C. Harrow,
tel: 0123 456 7891,
fax: 0123 456 7892,
email: c.harrow@ melchester.sch.uk.

I can be contacted at the above email address and could attend an interview at short notice.

Yours sincerely,
Lucy Johnson

If this is unsuccessful, you need to consider retaking your A levels and applying again (see below). The other alternative is to use the Clearing system to obtain a place on a degree course related to medicine and hope to apply to the medical course after you graduate.

Retaking your A levels

The grade requirements for retake candidates are normally higher than for first timers (usually AAA). You should retake any subject where your first result was below B and you should aim for an A grade in any subject you do retake. It is often necessary to retake a B grade, especially in Chemistry – take advice from the college that is preparing you for the retake.

Most AS and some A2 units can be taken in January sittings, and some boards offer other sittings. This means that a January retake is often technically possible, although you should check carefully before taking up this option, since there may be complications because of the number of times units/modules have already been taken, and because of coursework.

The timescale for your retake will depend on:

- the grades you obtained first time
- the syllabuses you studied.

If you simply need to improve one subject by one or two grades and can retake the exam on the same syllabus in January, then the short retake course is the logical option.

If, on the other hand, your grades were DDE and you took your exams through a board that has no mid-year retakes for the units that you require, you probably need to spend another year on your retakes. You would find it almost impossible to master syllabus changes in three subjects and achieve an increase of nine or 10 grades within the 17 weeks that are available for teaching between September and January.

Independent sixth-form colleges provide specialist advice and teaching for students considering A level retakes.

Interviews to discuss this are free and carry no obligation to enrol on a course, so it is worth taking the time to talk to their staff before you embark on A level retakes.

Reapplying to medical school

Many medical schools discourage retake candidates (see Table 8 on pages 134–5), so the whole business of applying again needs careful thought, hard work and a bit of luck. The choice of medical schools for your UCAS application is narrower than it was the first time round. Don't apply to the medical schools that discourage retakers unless there really are special, extenuating circumstances to explain your disappointing grades. Among the excuses that will not wash are:

- I wasn't feeling too good on the day of the practical exam, knocked over my Bunsen and torched the answer book
- my dog had been ill for a week before my exams and only recovered after the last paper (and I've got a vet's certificate to prove it)
- I'd spent the month before the exams condensing my notes on to small cards so that I could revise effectively. Two days before the exams, our house was broken into and the burglar trod on my notes as he climbed through the window. The police took them away for forensic examination and didn't give them back until after the last paper (and I've got a note from the CID to prove it).

Some reasons are acceptable to even the most fanatical opponents of retake candidates:

- your own illness
- the death or serious illness of a very close relative.

Consider, in addition, your age when you took the exams. Most medical schools will accept that a candidate who was well under the age of 18 on the date of sitting A levels may deserve another attempt without being branded a 'retaker'.

These are just guidelines, and the only safe method of finding out if a medical school will accept you is to ask them. Text for a typical email is set out below. Don't follow it slavishly and do take the time to write to several medical schools before you make your final choice.

To: Miss M. D. Whyte
Subject: Application to study Medicine at Melchester

Dear Miss Whyte
Last year's UCAS no. 08-123456-7

I am writing to ask your advice because I am about to complete my UCAS application and would very much like to apply to Melchester. You may remember that I applied to you last year and *received an offer of AAB/was rejected after interview/was rejected without an interview*. I have just received my A level results, which were:

Biology C, Chemistry D, English E.
I also have a B grade in AS Psychology.

I was aged 17 years and six months at the time of taking these exams. I plan to retake Chemistry in January after a 17-week course and English over a year. If necessary, I will retake Biology from January to June. I am confident that I can push these subjects up to A grades overall.

What worries me is that I have heard that some medical schools do not consider retake candidates even when the exams were taken under the age of 18 and relatively high grades were achieved. I am very keen not to waste a slot on my UCAS application (or your time) by applying to schools that will reject me purely because I am retaking. I am very keen to come to Melchester, and would be extremely grateful for any advice that you can give me.

Yours sincerely,
Lucy Johnson

Notice that the format of your email should be:

- opening paragraph
- your exam results – set out clearly and with no omissions
- any extenuating circumstances – a brief statement
- your retake plan – including the timescale

- a request for help and advice
- closing formalities.

Make sure that it is brief, clear and well presented. Apart from the care needed in making the choice of medical school, the rest of the application procedure is as described in the first section of this book.

05 Non-standard applications

So far, this book has been concerned with the 'standard' applicant: the UK resident who is studying at least two science subjects at A level and who is applying from school or who is retaking immediately after disappointing A levels. However, medical schools accept a small number of applicants who do not have this 'standard' background. The main non-standard categories are outlined in this chapter.

■ Those who have not studied science A levels

If you decide that you would like to study medicine after having already started on a combination of A levels that does not fit the subject requirements for entry to medical school, you can apply for the 'pre-medical course'.

The course covers elements of chemistry, biology and physics and lasts one academic year. It leads to the first MB qualification, for which science A levels provide exemption. If your pre-med application is rejected, you will have to spend a further two years taking science A levels at a sixth-form college. Alternatively, independent sixth-form colleges offer one-year A level courses, and certain subjects can be covered from scratch in a single year. However, only very able students can cover A level Chemistry and Biology in a single year with good results. You should discuss your particular circumstances with the staff of a number of colleges in order to select the course that will prepare you to achieve the A level subjects you need at the grades you require.

■ Overseas students

Most medical schools are limited by government quota to accepting only 7.5% of overseas students each year. In the academic year 2008/09 the tuition fees charged to these students were typically between £13,000 and £16,000 per year for the pre-clinical courses and between £21,000 and £28,000 and around £30,000 per year for the clinical courses.

Competition for the few places available to overseas students is fierce and you would be wise to discuss your application informally with the medical school before submitting your UCAS application. Many medical schools give preference to students who do not have adequate provision for training in their own countries. You should contact the medical schools individually for advice on application procedure and costs.

Information about qualifications can be obtained from British Council offices or British Embassies.

Mature students and graduates

Mature students

In recent years the options available for mature students have increased enormously. There is a growing awareness that older students often represent a 'safer' option for medical schools because they are likely to be more committed to medicine and less likely to drop out, and are able to bring to the medical world many skills and experiences that 18-year-olds sometimes lack. In general, there are two types of mature applicant:

1| those who have always wanted to study medicine but who failed to get into medical school when they applied from school in the normal way
2| those who came to the idea later on in life, often having embarked on a totally different career.

The first type of mature applicant has usually followed a degree course in a subject related to medicine and has obtained a good grade (minimum 2.1). These students have an uphill path into medicine because their early failure tends to prejudice the selectors. Nevertheless, they do not have the problem of taking science A levels at a late stage in their education. A few years ago, applicants in this position almost always had to go back to the beginning (sometimes even having to resit A levels) and then apply to the medical schools for the standard five-/six-year courses.

The second category of mature student is often of more interest to the medical school selectors and interviewers. Applications are welcomed from people who have achieved success in other careers and who can bring a breadth of experience to the medical school and to the profession.

Options available for mature students are summarised below. The chapter then examines each option in more detail.

Applicants with A levels that satisfy medical schools' standard offers
Five-/six-year courses in the normal way.

Applicants with A levels that do not satisfy standard offers

This could include arts A levels, or grades that are too low.

- Retake/pick up new A levels at sixth-form college.
- Six-year pre-medical/medical courses (First MB/ChB pre-medical entry) are available at:
  - Bristol
  - Cardiff
  - Dundee
  - Edinburgh
  - Keele
  - King's
  - Manchester
  - Sheffield
- These courses are usually given the code A104 by UCAS. They include a foundation (pre-medical) year and are designed for students without science A level backgrounds. They should not be confused with the six-year (usually A100) courses offered by many medical schools that include an intercalated BSc. The A100 courses require science A levels.
- Access courses.

Graduates

- Four-year graduate entry courses
- Five-/six-year courses in the normal way
- Six-year pre-medical/medical courses
- Access courses.

You should check which Access courses are accepted by medical schools. Not all will offer them. Often, each medical school has a short list of Access courses which it accepts applications from – for example at Keele they currently only look at Access courses from The Manchester College (previously called MANCAT), College of West Anglia, Sussex Downs Adult College, and University of Sussex at Brighton. Other medical schools accept different ones. It is also usually the case that you have to achieve very highly in these courses, not just pass them.

Mature students with no formal A level or equivalent qualifications

- A levels, then five-/six-year courses in the normal way
- Access courses.

Mature students and graduates are faced with many decisions on the route to becoming a doctor. Not only do they have to decide which course or combination of courses might be suitable, but in many cases they also have to try to gauge how best to juggle the conflicting demands of study, financial practicalities and their families.

Mature students need to prepare carefully for their applications in order to ensure that they are recognised as being fully committed to a career as a doctor. As an illustration of this, take the case of Matt Appleby.

Case study

Matt is a psychology graduate who is now studying A level Chemistry over a year. He applied to four medical schools and has offers from all of them. Matt writes:

It is unlikely that you will encounter something as uniquely stressful and as utterly absorbing as applying to medical school.

I say this not from the perspective of a 17-year-old A level student, I already did that once and it was arduous enough, but from the position of a 27-year-old graduate. For somebody serious about applying, the process should start at least a year beforehand.

Medical schools are immensely specific in what they want from their applicants. Your application may be inappropriate for one school, but desirable to another; each medical school likes to consider itself unique in its approach. Trust me; they will impress this upon you at interviews.

The best advice I got can be summed up simply: start early. Make contact with the admissions team. I emailed asking for more and more clarification, I took any opportunity to go to meet with the admissions staff. Quite a few places, such as King's, have an open door policy, which is fantastic. So when the day comes for an interview, or even maybe a rejection, you can show your determination through a paper trail.

I now know lots of people who've applied, and for every really impressive applicant I encounter, there are at least three or four who have applied to institutions for the wrong reasons; the city it is in or friends that are there. You have to go to as many open days as possible. This is usually your only opportunity to talk to admissions tutors directly – you can tell immediately from the conversation whether you should apply there or not on the basis of what the tutor or admissions officer says. I heard it all, from some downright outrageous hostility towards graduates such as myself, to really confidence-boosting remarks about my experience.

Creating a narrative

Getting an interview is easily the hardest part of the application process, but there is a strong correlation between preparation and your chances of getting it. I found that all the things admissions tutors are looking for can easily be demonstrated in a well-crafted UCAS state-ment. For instance, they always want to see the capacity to deal with stressful situations. So you want to show that you have really good coping mechanisms, something like sport, running, tai chi, whatever, but make a point of saying how it helps to deal with stress. They always ask this at interviews. Also show how you have been in stressful situations and survived. Don't give them an account of being mugged or the death of your beloved hamster, but go out and find an experience that actually tests you. Work as a much-needed volunteer in anything from soup kitchens to nursing homes. It does not need to be medically related, it just needs to show that you are made of tough stuff. They are pretty sick of hearing 'I shadowed a GP over half term'; everyone does it, I did it, and all it tends to show is your capacity to be a nuisance.

Admissions staff are always going to want to see experience, but it is all about what that experience meant to you. They seem to be far more impressed by somebody who gave an evening a week working with underprivileged children than someone who ran around behind their dad's best mate who is fortunately a top neurosurgeon. Shadowing is important to show only because it gives an insight into the workings of the NHS. Far more salient are the experiences of an applicant who performs a meaningful and thought-provoking responsibility.

The art of creating this 'narrative' is in showing that you have really considered medicine carefully. You need to demonstrate the time and planning that has gone into your decision and how you have gone about accruing the necessary experiences. Without this you will be sunk in the water. That's not to say that you can't get some things together quickly. I shadowed a psychiatrist, an anaesthetist and signed up for volunteering at my local hospice all in the space of a few weeks. But these experiences are only what you make of them. Your aim is to create the story of your experience, your acdemic record and your capacity to bring all your great qualities to their medical school. Don't be shy. It is ruthless self-promotion.

Interviews

My biggest enemy was stress. You have been contemplating the interview for months before you even started applying, and now, in your head, it's all or nothing. For my first interview I was almost bouncing off the walls. There were so many things I wanted to say, and as the words came out of my mouth there was almost an out of body experience – like seeing yourself in the third person, trying des-perately to make every point count. The only advice I can give to you about coping with the stress was what was given to me – breathe and try and keep a sense of perspective.

It is an interview, and you may think it is all or nothing, but you've got this far. It was not a fluke, you had something in your application, your experiences, or your grades that made them say, 'let's hear a little more from this one'.

You know it is coming, and yet, when asked, it immediately seems to bamboozle you: 'So Matt, why do you want to be a doctor?'

Prepare for this question right now. Your interviewers know that you have prepared for this question, but they really do not seem to like answers that are clearly rehearsed. If you make your answer sound too practised then they will just fire questions at you until they break into something you didn't prepare for. You don't want this. I was asked what I thought the greatest stressors were on junior doctors, and I started firing off the prepared answers; MTAS, long hours, working nights, dealing with death on a daily basis. But they were not happy until I had run out of answers, and actually was forced to sit and really think. The interviewers are impressed with a candidate who has prepared, but they also want a doctor who can think on his feet. In all the interviews I have had they asked questions that stumped me. Let's face it, you have three or even four highly trained clinicians and practitioners interviewing you; it is right that they should be really testing. It is a cliché, but I don't care – this really is your opportunity to sell yourself. Enjoy it!

There are not always questions from medical stories in the newspapers, but I have been asked about a story that was pertinent to my personal statement. There are many medical schools that tell you in advance that you will have to consider an ethical case. For this, the best preparation is to buy a short introductory medical ethics book and take some brief notes. It is impressive when being asked an ethical question on joint replacement for you to be able offer different perspectives. Medical ethics came up in every interview I had, and I was glad for the hours of work I'd put in. It's an interesting subject anyway.

As I was a psychology graduate, I was always being asked why I didn't want to be a psychologist. As a graduate they also always ask 'Why now?' 'Why not earlier?' 'What has made you change direction?' I gave an earnest answer but in my modest opinion, keep the emotional stuff to a minimum. Interviewers do not want to hear about a life-changing event when you broke your arm or even something as sad as a death in the family. I had been working as an ambulance medic overseas and had many an emotional experience that drove me ever closer to medicine, but first and foremost I find the subject matter compelling. I am interested, I want to learn more. I want to do a job that is both financially rewarding and fulfilling. I am aware of the years of work and study and financial responsibility, and I have made a qualified and clear decision to pursue this course. This is what they want to hear.

After the interview

I remember walking out of at least two interviews and thinking the best I had done was simply okay, and I walked out of another thinking it had gone terribly. The fact is that none of these appraisals was correct. The one that had gone the worst was the institution that gave me the best offer. You just do not know what is going on in the heads of the interviewers. It is not that they are a miserable bunch of doctors, but they have a considerable responsibility and do not take it lightly. The best advice I can suggest is an insight from a professor of law I know who regularly interviews judges, postgraduates and undergraduate students. She is always nice, no matter what she thinks of the candidate. It just makes her life easier and the process more pleasant for all parties involved, but I can imagine there are many candidates who walk out thinking 'that went swimmingly, I can't believe she laughed at my joke', only to later find themselves unsuccessful.

Matt's medical-school interview questions were typical of those faced by mature students and graduates. The interviewers were interested in:

- why he had decided to change direction
- what he had done to convince himself that this was the right option for him
- what his career had given him in the way of personal qualities that were relevant to medicine
- what financial arrangements he had made to fund his studies
- whether he had found it difficult studying A levels alongside 18-year-olds.

Personal statement

Take your personal statement to as many sensible people who know what they are talking about as you can. Bribe teachers with coffee and chocolate. Go to science teachers for help, as the people reading the finished article tend to see things from a similar rationale; along the lines of 'Why is that there?' and 'What's the point of saying that? It's just waffle.' Keep the writing simple, don't overuse the thesaurus, and check spelling and punctuation to ridiculous extremes. Remember, spell check isn't foolproof and won't flag the difference between principle and principal, or effect and affect. It's the little things like that which could ruin a perfectly good application.

For mature applicants, the UCAS personal statement needs to be carefully structured. In most cases, insufficient space is allowed for the amount of information necessary to present a convincing case. It is usually advisable for mature applicants to send a detailed CV and covering letter direct to the medical schools once their UCAS number has been received.

For mature applicants, the personal statement should be structured as follows:

1| brief career and educational history – in note form or bullet points if necessary
2| reasons for the change of direction
3| what the candidate has done to investigate medicine
4| brief details of achievements, interests, etc. – again, note form or bullet points are fine.

The most important thing to bear in mind is that you must convince the selectors that you are serious about the change in direction, and that your decision to apply to study medicine is not a spur-of-the-moment reaction to dissatisfaction with your current job or studies.

A useful exercise is to try to imagine that you are the person who will read the personal statement in order to decide whether to interview or to reject without interview. Does your personal statement contain sufficient indication of thorough research, preparation and long-term commitment? If it does not, you will be rejected. As a rough guide, at least half of it should cover your reasons for applying for a medical course and the preparation and research that you have undertaken. The further back in time you can demonstrate that you started to plan your application, the stronger it will be.

■ Doing a pre-medical course

Pre-medical courses or programmes are not to be confused with Access courses. As the name suggests, pre-medical courses usually act as a 'pre-medical school year' or 'year zero' before you enter medical school. The best-known of these is the M&D Pre-Medical Programme run at the University of Sussex. This programme is unique because is aims to secure a place in a UK medical school with the added security of securing a place in an overseas medical school.

Each year, a number of students on this programme, who may have previously applied for medicine in the UK, secure a place in a UK medical school. Those that don't are offered a place in the first or second year at medical degree courses in Slovakia, the Czech Republic, Poland and the Caribbean. (See 'Studying outside the UK', below). Students who do not secure a place in a UK medical school or choose not to continue with medicine can move into the second year of a life science degree course in the UK.

See www.mdpremed.com for more details.

■ Access courses

A number of colleges of further education offer Access to Medicine courses. The best-known and most successful of these is the course at the College of West Anglia, in King's Lynn. Primarily (but not exclusively) aimed at health professionals, the course covers biology, chemistry, physics and other medically related topics, and lasts one year. Most medical schools will accept students who have successfully completed the course. Contact details can be found at the end of the book.

■ Four-year graduate courses

Often known as GEPs (Graduate Entry Programmes), these are given the code A101 or A102 by UCAS. The biggest change in medical school entry in recent years has been the development of these graduate entry schemes. The first medical schools to introduce accelerated courses specifically for graduates were St George's Hospital Medical School and Leicester/Warwick (which has since split into two separate medical schools). Courses can be divided into two types:

1| those for graduates with a medically related degree
2| those that accept graduates with degrees in any discipline.

About 10% of UK medical school placements are now on GEPs. The following medical schools run GEPs (UCAS code A101/A102), further details of which can be found on the UCAS website:

- Birmingham
- Bristol
- Cambridge
- Imperial
- Keele
- King's
- Leicester
- Liverpool
- Newcastle
- Nottingham
- Oxford
- Queen Mary
- Southampton
- St George's
- Swansea
- Warwick.

The King's course differs from the others listed above, as it is also available to healthcare professionals with equivalent academic qualifications. The first year of the course is taught in London or in Kent. Students then join the other King's MB BS students for the remaining three years.

GAMSAT

Four medical schools use the GAMSAT (Graduate Australian Medical School Admissions Test). For GAMSAT enquiries, email gamsat@ucas.ac.uk or see www.gamsat.co.uk.

> Standard Registrations for the GAMSAT UK test to be held on 17 September 2010 will open on **Friday 4 June 2010** and will close **midnight (GMT) Friday 13 August 2010**. The fee to sit the GAMSAT test is £192. Payment must be made by credit card at the time of completing your online registration or by bank draft after completing a provisional registration. No other payment options are available.
>
> Late registrations will be accepted up to **midnight (GMT) Friday 27 August 2010**, on payment of a **late fee of £50** in addition to the registration fee.

Candidates sit the GAMSAT examination in September, and those with the best all-round scores are then called for interview. The GAMSAT examination consists of three papers:

1| reasoning in humanities and social sciences (75 multiple-choice questions)
2| written communication (two essays)
3| reasoning in biological and physical sciences (110 multiple-choice questions: 40% biology, 40% chemistry, 20% physics).

The medical schools that use the GAMSAT examination for their graduate courses are:

- Keele
- Nottingham
- St George's
- Swansea.

Peninsula also uses the GAMSAT for anyone who has not sat A levels in the last two years. Peninsula does not offer the A101 course.

Studying outside the UK

If you are unsuccessful in gaining a place at one of the UK medical schools, and do not want to follow the graduate-entry path, you might want to look at other options. One option for those who have been unsuccessful with their applications is to study medicine abroad – for example at Charles University in the Czech Republic or Comenius University in Bratislava, capital of Slovakia. There are a number of medical schools throughout the world that will accept A level students, but the important issue is whether or not you would be able, should you wish to do so, to practise in the UK upon qualification. These five- to six-year courses are taught in English, and graduates are recognised in the UK by the General Medical Council.

Courses often attended by UK students include the following.

- St George's University School of Medicine in Grenada (West Indies) (the most popular and 'tried and tested' option, for those who can afford the fees). Students who wish to practise in the UK can spend part of the clinical stage of the course in a range of hospitals in the UK, including King's in London. To practise in the UK, students sit the PLAB (Professional and Linguistic Assessments Board) test to gain limited registration; for more information, see www.gmc-uk. org/doctors/plab/index.asp. Clinical experience can also be gained in hospitals in the US, allowing students to practise there as well. A high proportion of the St George's University medical school teachers have worked in UK universities and medical schools.
- Four-year medical degree courses at St Matthew's University, Grand Cayman. The first two years are taught on Grand Cayman (British West Indies) and the final two clinical years are taught in the UK or the US. This course will consider science graduates or those that have successfully passed the one-year M&D Pre-Medical Programme. The European Applications office can be found at www. studymedicine.co.uk.
- Six-year medical degree courses in Slovakia, the Czech Republic and Poland. These courses are taught in English and are recognised in the UK. In some cases, students may be considered for second year entry if they have completed the M&D Pre-medical Programme. Applications can be made via www.readmedicine.com.
- Medical courses taught in English at Charles University in Prague and at other universities in the Czech Republic.

It is advisable for anyone applying for UK medical schools that they have a back-up option to study medicine in Europe, in the event that their application for the UK is unsuccessful. As applications are made via M&D Europe and not via UCAS, applicants who are offered a place to study medicine in Europe are not obliged to accept their place if they choose to study in the UK.

Applicants who have completed up to science A level standard (or equivalent) are invited for an entrance examination, usually in April of each year in London, held by M&D Europe. Applicants who have already completed their A levels may be exempted from this examination.

The M&D Pre-Med Programme run at the University of Sussex usually confirms a place to study medicine in European countries if applicants are unsuccessful in securing a place at a UK medical school. Although the M&D Pre-Med Programme is run predominantly for medical students, some UK dental schools have agreed to consider and accept students from this programme. See www.mdpremed.com for more details.

In addition to the medical schools attached to UK universities, there are a number of institutions offering medical degree courses that are taught in the UK but are accredited by overseas universities – mostly based in the Caribbean, Russia or Africa. If you are considering these, you must ensure that you are fully satisfied that the courses are bona fide and that the qualification you receive will allow you to practise in the UK (or anywhere else in the world!). Details of these medical schools can be found in Chapter 9.

Getting into US medical schools

Here I can only point those who are interested in studying medicine in the US in the right direction. Principally, what you will need to do is go to the AAMC (Association of American Medical Colleges) website. This is an excellent site, but dense. All the member universities are listed, and by following links, most of your questions can be answered. Furthermore, from here you can be directed to AMCAS, which is the American Medical College Application Service for students who wish to apply. The website for AAMC is www.aamc.org, and for students wishing to apply, go to www.aamc.org/students/start.htm.

The AAMC website suggests that a very good investment is the *Medical School Admission Requirements (MSAR) 2009–2010* book, published in April 2008, which can be bought for $25, also known as the 'bible of medical school guides'.

Another source of information is the Trotman guide *Getting Into US and Canadian Universities* by Margaret Kroto. This is a very useful book as it gives an overview of the difficulties, and procedures necessary to gain entry. This, however, is a more generalist guide for entry.

Suffice it to say here that the following criteria have to be met.

- You are expected to gain very high grades in AS/A levels – nearly all straight A grades. The higher the grades, the higher your GPA (Grade Point Average) will be. An A grade = 4 GPA points; a B grade = 3; and a B+ = 3.75. Thus, a high GPA will improve your chances of being selected by the more renowned universities.
- You will be expected to sit SAT entrance tests (formerly Scholastic Aptitude Test and Scholastic Assessment Test) – these are standardised tests for college admissions in the US.
- The current SAT Reasoning Test is administered in about four hours and costs $45 (£27.60) ($71 (£43.60) for international students), excluding late fees (as of 4 July 2008).
- You will be asked to provide two or three references from your personal tutor and teachers.
- If you are not from an English-speaking country you will be required to sit a TOEFL test in which the minimum score for entry into any university is 550 points. The more demanding the course (such as

medicine) and the more prestigious the university, the higher this language requirement will be.

■ Most universities accept the British IELTS, but it must be 7 points or above.

■ Both the SAT and the TOEFL tests can be sat in the UK.

■ Fees and living costs are very high. A full list can be obtained from the AAMC website.

If you are very serious about applying, you need to start as early as possible – early in the AS level year is recommended. This is because you will need to research the universities as best you can, bearing in mind that the distance does not allow for quick visits to open days as for UK universities.

In the US, medicine is a postgraduate degree. All students enter the schools after doing two years of undergraduate study. In these first two years you can study something different, but you must obviously study a science-based or pre-med course. Also expected in these first two years is gaining work experience. For more information go to www. aamc.org/students/considering/timeline.htm.

06 Careers in medicine

This chapter looks briefly at some of the possible routes open to prospective medics. It is of value to have an idea and indeed some understanding of the possibilities and avenues open to you both while you are studying and for the interview. Arguably some knowledge here could be of great benefit if you are asked 'have you given any thought to future prospects' or, 'where do you see yourself in 10 years' type questions.

The number of paths and avenues open to members of the medical profession once they graduate are numerous and too many to go into in detail here. As a trainee doctor nearing the end of your study, questions such as the prospect and possibility of specialisation and of where you might like to work have to be answered. The best advice I can give here is to make sure to research as much as possible, talk to people and, above all, be aware of the areas in medicine that you have enjoyed the most.

Apart from specialisations (see below), there is a wide range of areas that doctors may end up working in. Obviously, most people understand that many doctors become GPs. However, there are also as many who dedicate their lives to working in the state-funded NHS. Within the NHS there is a panoply of possibilities such as working in public health, working in medical management and administration and even working in research.

Away from public hospitals, there are careers to be made in private enterprise, for example running a consultancy business such as plastic surgery. Some doctors opt for the armed forces and others work for the police as forensic psychiatrists and forensic pathologists.

Another area is education, in terms of lecturing, research and writing whilst working for a university. It is not uncommon to find doctors who have a portfolio of work, spending some of their time in hospitals, doing private consultancy in their own surgeries and teaching or doing research. Such a life is not only well remunerated but also stimulating.

First job

The training programme for doctors called Modernising Medical Careers (MMC) became fully functional in 2007. The reforms to medical training were proposed in 2002, primarily to remedy the problems within the

Senior House Officer (SHO) grade, particularly in regard to the lack of a structured training programme and career path, which many doctors felt was absent. Before the MMC, newly qualified doctors would spend a year at Pre-registration House Officer level, dividing the period between medicine and surgery. After that, the junior doctor would be working as an SHO for a number of years before applying for a Specialist Registrar post.

MMC is summarised in Figure 2.

In the last year of the medical degree, medical students apply for a place on the Foundation programme. The Foundation programme is designed to provide structured postgraduate training on the job and lasts two years. The job starts a few weeks after graduating from medical school. In the first few weeks there might be a short period of 'shadowing', to help new doctors get used to the job. After successful completion of the first year, they will gain registration with the GMC.

The Foundation programme job is divided into three four-month posts in the first year. These posts will typically consist of:

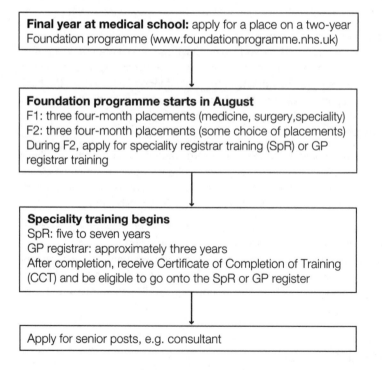

Figure 2 Modernising Medical Careers training structure

- four months of surgery (e.g. urology, general surgery)
- four months of another speciality (e.g. psychiatry, GP or anything else)
- four months in a medical speciality (e.g. respiratory, geriatrics).

The second year is again divided into three four-month posts, but here the focus is perhaps on a speciality or may include other jobs in shortage areas.

For more information on the application procedure, visit www.medschoolsonline.co.uk/index.php?pageid=157 and www.foundationprogramme.nhs.uk.

Specialisations

Specialist training programmes typically last for five to seven years. After gaining the CCT, a doctor is then eligible to apply for a Certificate of Eligibility for Specialist Registration (CESR). Either will make you eligible for entry to the GMC's Specialist Register or GP Register.

To do this you will need to apply for postgraduate medical training programmes in the UK with the deanery or 'unit of application' directly. In this application process you will be competing for places on speciality training programmes with other doctors at similar levels of competence and experience.

For more information, visit the PMETB website at www.pmetb.org.uk.

Here follow the 10 major specialisations available in medicine, each with its own sub-specialisations and some selected elaborations:

1| accident and emergency
2| anaesthetics
3| general practice
4| intensive care
5| medical specialities
- cardiovascular disease
- clinical genetics
- clinical pharmacology and therapeutics
- dermatology
- endocrinology and diabetes mellitus
- gastroenterology
- general medicine
- genito-urinary medicine
- geriatrics
- infectious diseases
- medical oncology
- nephrology (renal medicine)
- neurology
- occupational medicine
- paediatrics

- □ palliative medicine
- □ rehabilitation medicine
- □ rheumatology
- □ tropical medicine
6| obstetrics and gynaecology
7| pathology
- □ bacteriology
- □ blood transfusion
- □ chemical pathology
- □ diagnostic radiology
- □ forensic pathology
- □ haematology
- □ histopathology
- □ immunology
- □ medical microbiology
- □ neuropathology
- □ radiology
- □ radiology and nuclear medicine
- □ radiotherapy
8| psychiatry
- □ adult psychiatry
- □ child and adolescent psychiatry
- □ forensic psychiatry
- □ old age psychiatry
- □ psychiatry of learning difficulties
9| public health medicine
- □ clinical public health
- □ government medical service
- □ medical administration
10| surgical specialities
- □ general surgery
- □ neurosurgery
- □ ophthalmology
- □ otolaryngology
- □ paediatric surgery
- □ plastic surgery
- □ thoracic surgery
- □ urology.

Below are a few selected specialisations, which are briefly described.

Anaesthetist

An anaesthetist is a medical doctor trained to administer anaesthesia and manage the medical care of patients before, during and after surgery. Anaesthetists are the single largest group of hospital doctors and their skills are used throughout the hospital in patient care. They have a medical background to deal with many emergency situations.

They are also trained to deal with breathing, resuscitation of the heart and lungs and advanced life support.

Audiologist

Audiologists identify and assess hearing and/or balance disorders, and from this will recommend and provide appropriate rehabilitation for the patient. The main areas of work are paediatrics, adult assessment and rehabilitation, special needs groups and research and development.

Cardiologist

This is the branch of medicine that deals with disorders of the heart and blood vessels. Physicians specialising in this field are called cardiologists.

These specialists deal with the diagnosis and treatment of heart defects, heart failure and valvular heart disease.

Dermatologist

There are over 2,000 recognised diseases of the skin but about 20 of these account for 90% of the workload. Dermatologists are specialist physicians who diagnose and treat diseases of the skin, hair and nails such as severe acne in teenagers, which happens to be a very common reason for referral. Inflammatory skin diseases such as eczema and psoriasis are very common and without treatment can produce significant disability.

Gastroenterologist

A gastroenterologist is a medically qualified specialist who has subspecialised in the diseases of the digestive system, which include ailments affecting all organs, from mouth to anus, along the alimentary canal. In all, a gastroenterologist undergoes a minimum of 13 years of formal classroom education and practical training before becoming a certified gastroenterologist.

General practitioner (GP)

A GP is a medical practitioner who specialises in family medicine and primary care. They are often referred to as family doctors and work in consultation clinics based in the local community.

GPs can work on their own or in a group practice with other doctors and healthcare providers. A GP treats acute and chronic illnesses and provides care and health education for all ages. They are called GPs because they look after a whole person, and this includes their mental health and physical well-being.

Gynaecologist

Gynaecologists have a broad base of knowledge and can vary their professional focus on different disorders and diseases of the female reproductive system. This includes preventative care, prenatal care and detection of sexually transmitted diseases, Pap test screening and family planning. They may choose to specialise in different areas, such as acute and chronic medical conditions, for example cervical cancer, infertility, urinary tract disorders and pregnancy and delivery.

Immunologist

Immunologists are responsible for investigating the functions of the body's immune system. They help to treat diseases like AIDS, allergies (e.g. asthma, hay fever) and leukaemia using complex and sophisticated molecular techniques. They deal with the understanding of the processes and effects of inappropriate stimulation that are associated with allergies and transplant rejection, and may be heavily involved with research. An immunologist works within clinical and academic settings as well as with industrial research. Their role involves measuring components of the immune system, including cells, antibodies and other proteins. They develop new therapies, which involves looking at how to improve methods for treating different conditions.

Neurologist

A neurologist is a medical doctor who has trained in the diagnosis and treatment of nervous system disorders, which includes diseases of the brain, spinal cord, nerves and muscles. Neurologists perform medical examinations of the nerves of the head and neck; muscle strength and movement, balance, ambulation and reflexes, memory, speech, language and other cognitive abilities.

Obstetrician

These are specialised doctors who deal with problems that arise during maternity care, treating any complications that develop in pregnancy and childbirth and any that arise after the birth. Some obstetricians may specialise in a particular aspect of maternity care such as maternal medicine, which involves looking after the mother's health; labour care, which involves care during the birth; and/or fetal medicine, which involves looking after the health of the unborn baby,

Paediatrician

This is a physician who deals with the growth, development and health of children from birth to adolescence. To become a paediatrician doctors must complete six years of extra training after they finish their medical training. There are general paediatricians and specialist paediatricians such as paediatric cardiologists. They work in private practices or hospitals.

Plastic surgeon

Plastic surgery is the medical and cosmetic speciality that involves the correction of form and function. There are two main types of plastic surgery: cosmetic and reconstructive.

1| Cosmetic surgery procedures alter a part of the body that the person is not satisfied with, such as breast implants or fat removal.
2| Reconstructive plastic surgery, on the other hand, includes correcting defects on the face or body – these may include physical birth defects, such as cleft palates or the aftermath of disease treatments, such as disfigurement after a fire.

Plastic surgery includes a variety of fields such as hand surgery, burn surgery, microsurgery and paediatric surgery.

Psychiatrist

Psychiatrists are trained in the medical, psychological and social components of mental, emotional and behavioural disorders. They specialise in the prevention and diagnosis and treatment of mental, addictive and emotional disorders such as anxiety, depression, psychosis, substance abuse and developmental disabilities. They prescribe medications, practise psychotherapy and help patients and their families cope with stress and crises. Psychiatrists often consult with primary care physicians, psychotherapists, psychologists and social workers.

Surgeon

A general surgeon is a physician who has been educated and trained in diagnosis, operative and post-operative treatment, and management of patient care. Surgery requires extensive knowledge of anatomy, emergency and intensive care, nutrition, pathology, shock and resuscitation, and wound healing. Surgeons may practise in specific fields such as general surgery, orthopaedic, neurological or vascular and many more.

Urologist

A urologist is a physician who has specialised knowledge and skills regarding problems of the male and female urinary tract and the male reproductive organs. Extensive knowledge of internal medicine, paediatrics, gynaecology and other specialities is required by the urologist.

Some alternative careers

Armed Forces

Doctors in the Army are also officers, and provide medical care for soldiers and their families (www.mod.uk/DefenceInternet/DefenceFor/jobseekers).

Aviation medicine (also aerospace medicine)

The main role is to assess the fitness to fly of pilots, cabin crew and infirm passengers (www.facoccmed.ac.uk).

Clinical forensic medical examiner (police surgeon)

Clinical forensic physicians/medical examiners spend much of their time examining people who have been arrested. Detainees either ask to see a doctor, or need to be examined to see if they are fit for interview or fit to be detained (www.forensic-science-society.org.uk).

Coroner

The coroner is responsible for inquiring into violent, sudden and unexpected, unnatural or suspicious deaths. Few are doctors, but some have qualifications in both medicine and law (see the section on clinical forensic and legal medicine of the Royal Society of Medicine: www.rsm.ac.uk).

Pharmaceutical medicine

Job opportunities for doctors in pharmaceutical medicine include clinical research, medical advisory positions and becoming the medical director of a company. Patient contact is limited but still possible in the clinical trials area (www.abpi.org.uk).

Prison medicine

A prison medical officer provides healthcare, usually in the form of GP clinics, to prison inmates (www.cblocums.co.uk/cm/locums/prisons).

Public health practitioner

Public health medicine is a speciality that deals with health at the level of a general population rather than at the level of the individual. The role can vary from responding to outbreaks of disease that need a rapid response, such as food poisoning, to the long-term planning of health-care (www.fphm.org.uk).

07 Fees and funding

To find out the fees and funding for medical courses, prospective students should explore each of the universities' websites and/or talk to the universities' financial departments. This is because fees and funding procedures vary from university to university.

Whether undertaking undergraduate or postgraduate studies, the costs can be considerable. According to the BMA Survey of Medical Student Finances 2008/09:

> Almost all respondents reported some level of credit card, bank loan, student loan or overdraft debt. Respondents in their final year of study (defined as those expecting to graduate in 2009) reported an average level of total debt of £22,821 with the highest level of total debt reported as £65,941. This in an increase of 20% since 2007/08. The average loan amount for tuition fees for respondents in their first year of study was more than double that for fifth year respondents when they were in their first year of study. 35 per cent and 45 per cent of respondents in their fifth and sixth year of study respectively reported a level of overall debt greater than £25,000. 84 per cent of total debt was accounted for by outstanding student loan debt, which includes loans for tuition and maintenance.

Source: www.bma.org.uk/careers/medical_education/
student_finance/studentfinancesurveys.jsp

Bear in mind that the difference depends on so many factors. Factors affecting the overall debt can include: geographic – does the student live in a city? the amount of help that parents can give; if the student receives a scholarship; and/or if the student has found work. Whatever the circumstances, a student must give serious consideration to the cost and be prepared to fully commit. It also has to involve careful financial planning for the four or five years that a course may last. On top of the tuition fees, students will also have to consider living costs; needless to say, in big cities like London, living costs will be much higher than in other parts of the country. One estimate is that London will cost about £9,000 per year to cover food, accommodation, travel and books.

Fees for international students

Home students – that is, UK nationals – and EU students pay lower tuition fees than non-EU/UK students. For international students outside of these two regions, the costs can be prohibitive. In Barts and The London School of Medicine and Dentistry (part of Queen Mary), for example, the fees given for home-grown and EU students are £3,000 per year, which can be taken on as a loan. While this is substantial (and it adds up over a five-year course), it is still nowhere near the expense incurred by overseas students. The 2009 tuition fees for Medicine (A100) were £15,350 per year in Years 1 and 2, increasing to £24,000 per year for tuition in Years 3, 4 and 5. This is envisaged to go up in 2010 (figures taken from www.qmul.ac.uk/international/feesfinance/index.html).

To use another example, this time at Peninsula University, the fees for overseas students in the academic year 2008/09 are as follows:

- Years 1 and 2: £13,000
- Years 3, 4 and 5: £20,500 (figures taken from www.pms.ac.uk/pms/undergraduate/international.php).

Nevertheless, whether you are a UK/EU resident or an overseas student, the truth of the matter is that unless you are wealthy, the average and usual scenario is that you will accumulate a large debt. Again, according to the BMA, in 2007 an average accrual of debt followed as shown below. These figures show the overall average debt by year of study, primarily made up of student loan debt:

- £7,776 for first years
- £9,953 for second years
- £13,820 for third years
- £17,439 for fourth years
- £18,524 for fifth years
- £21,057 for sixth years.

Student grants

Home student grants can help with the paying of tuition fees but this depends on an assessment made by the local authority based on how much your parents earn. A student will only get a full grant if the assessment comes in at £25,000 or less.

Student loans

The most common way that students are able to fund themselves is by taking out a student loan. Students can take out two types of loan: loan for fees and loan for living costs. Students will only start repaying these loans once they have finished studying and are earning over £15,000 per year. Most universities can put you in touch with loan agencies and with the NHS.

▓ NHS bursaries

NHS bursaries are available for full- and part-time students. To be eligible for such a bursary a student must qualify as a 'home student' and be on a course that is accepted as an NHS-funded place. These bursaries will be available for medical students, as medical degrees are recognised as an NHS-funded course. For more information, the NHS student grants unit website at www.nhsstudentgrants.co.uk is useful. It is also worth finding out from universities if scholarships are available. According to the NHS website, in the 2008/09 academic year, the Department of Health agreed to pay the tuition fee contribution for each student affected, up to a maximum amount of £3,145. This amount cannot be exceeded under any circumstances, and therefore if a university charges higher fees than this amount in the academic year, students will be expected to meet the balance themselves.

▓ How to apply for financial support: UK students

New students in England

- ▓ Ask for an application form from the Local Authority (LA) in whose area you normally live.
- ▓ Ask for an application form from the Student Loan Company (SLC) if you live in an area testing the new finance arrangements.
- ▓ Apply online/download a form (Form PN1).

New students in Northern Ireland

- ▓ Ask for an application form from the Education and Library Board (ELB) in whose area you normally live.
- ▓ Apply online/download a form (Form PN1).

New students in Wales

- ▓ Apply to the LA in whose area you normally live.
- ▓ Apply online/download a form (Form PN1).

New students in Scotland

- ▓ Apply to the Student Awards Agency for Scotland (SAAS) wherever you live in Scotland.
- ▓ Apply online/download a form (Form SAS3).

According to Money4Medstudents (www.money4medstudents.org/content.asp?id=502), the following changes were made to funding for 2008/09:

- increases in the household income threshold for the full maintenance grant for new students in England from £17,000 to £25,000 with a partial grant being available up to a household income of £60,005 – for a student from a family on £40,000 per annum, this will mean a grant of about £1,000
- repayment holidays on student loans for students from England due to start repayment of their loan from April 2012
- major changes to income assessment for new and continuing students from Scotland
- increases in the Disabled Students' Allowances.

At the time of writing, up-to-date information for 2009/10 was not available. Keep an eye on the Money4Medstudents website for any further changes.

Other sources of funding for medical student projects

There are various websites that will give you information on a variety of organisations that can offer scholarships, grants and bursaries that are in addition to the NHS bursary. These include:

- **Access Agreement bursaries:** non-repayable bursaries, typically for £310 upwards, for students receiving the full Maintenance Grant/Special Support Grant (except in Scotland, where a fee waiver/bursary scheme may be an alternative for students from Scotland)
- **Armed Forces bursaries/cadetships:** these are generous and may be worth considering, provided you are happy to commit to an agreed number of years working as a doctor in the Army, Navy or Air Force
- **medical awards and competitions:** these are of varying amounts and varying levels of competitiveness
- **university bursaries:** many universities often provide bursaries for low-income students. If your household income is below £17,910 you will probably receive a bursary of at least £305. However, some bursaries are more than this and some universities give bursaries to people with higher incomes. It is worth investigating this with your university
- **hardship loans:** if you are having financial problems you can apply for additional sources of funding; up to £500 can be added on to your current student loan.

For more information on these, go to www.medschoolsonline.co.uk/index.php?pageid=224 and www.aimhigher.ac.uk/Uni4me/what_will_it_cost_/is_there_other_money_available_o_help_me_/university_bursaries__grants_and_sponsorships.cfm.

There are also many scholarships and prizes that are run by the many professional medical organisations. Some of these applications may require a supporting statement from a member of academic staff. Check criteria carefully before applying.

- **British Association of Dermatologists.** Offers £5,000 towards fees and living expenses for an intercalated-year project related to dermatology and skin biology. It also offers £500 as undergraduate project grants.
- **Sir John Ellis Student Prizes.** Students submit a description of a piece of work, survey, research or innovation in which they have been directly involved, in the field of medical education. First Prize in each category is £300 plus expenses (conference fee, accommodation in Halls of Residence, Annual Dinner and standard travel expenses). Runners up will have the conference fee and accommodation in the Halls of Residence paid for.
- **The Genetics Society.** The Genetics Society Summer Studentship scheme provides funding for undergraduate students to spend their summer vacation working in a genetics laboratory in order to gain research experience.
- **The Nuffield Foundation.** A scheme similar to The Genetics Society Summer Studentship is also run by the Nuffield Foundation.
- **The Physiological Society.** Offers grants of up to £1,200 for students undertaking research of a physiologic nature under the supervision of a member of the society during a summer vacation or intercalated BSc year (if not receiving LA or other government support).
- **The Pathological Society.** Offers funding for students wanting to intercalate a BSc in Pathology but who do not have LA or other government support. Also offers awards to fund electives and vacation studies in pathology.

08 Current issues

It is obviously impossible to know about all illnesses and issues in medicine. However, being aware of some of the contemporary issues in medicine today will be of enormous benefit, particularly if you are asked, as many candidates are, to extrapolate and elucidate on 'an issue' in an interview. Showing that you have an awareness of issues on more than a passing or superficial level demonstrates intelligence, interest and enthusiasm for medicine.

This will undoubtedly stand you in good stead next to a candidate who is either very hazy or is at worst completely unaware of a major issue in medicine. The following section illustrates, albeit briefly, some of the major issues that are currently causing debate, both in medical circles and in wider society. A little bit of awareness and knowledge can go a long way to securing and leaving a positive impression on an interview board. This section is to be read with an eye to some of the exemplar questions given in Chapter 3.

National Health Service

This is a very topical issue, and one that has elicited a lot of negative comments from practitioners. It is a very common area of questioning by interview teams.

The National Health Service (NHS) was set up in 1948 to provide healthcare free of charge at the point of delivery. That is not to say that, if you fell ill in 1947, you necessarily had to pay for your treatment.

Accident and emergency services had been developed and had coped well with the demands of a population under bombardment during the Second World War. Some hospitals were ancient, wealthy, charitable institutions owning valuable assets such as property in London. These hospitals charged patients who could afford to pay and treated others without charge. Doctors often worked on the same basis. Other hospitals were owned and funded by local authorities. The system was supported by low-cost insurance schemes, which were often fully or partially funded by employers.

The problem perceived by the architects of the NHS was that poorer members of society were reluctant to seek diagnosis and treatment. By funding the system out of a national insurance scheme to which every employer and employee would contribute, the government conferred on all citizens (whether employed or not) the right to free healthcare without the stigma of charity.

The service has undergone a number of reforms since 1948, but by far the most fundamental was introduced by the Conservative government in 1990. In recent years, the Labour government has made further changes to the system. It is important to understand what these reforms were, why they were thought to be necessary and what the outcome has been.

By the late 1980s it was clear to the government that the NHS could not function in the future without a substantial increase in funding. The fundamental reason for this was an expected reduction in the taxpayer's contribution, linked to an anticipated increase in demand for healthcare. Let's see why this was so.

Increased demand

By 1990:

- the NHS had become a victim of its own success. When the service saved the life of a patient who would normally have died, that person survived to have another illness, to receive more treatment and incur more expense for the NHS
- the number of life-prolonging procedures/treatments/drugs had increased as a result of developments in medical science
- the cost of these sophisticated procedures/treatments/drugs was high, and increasing at a rate faster than inflation
- the cost of staff had increased because, while pay rates had risen, the hours worked for that pay had fallen. At the same time, the cost of training staff in the new procedures and equipment was high
- patient expectations had grown – knowledge of the new procedures/treatment/drugs meant that patients demanded access to them without delay.

The 1990 reforms

The government believed that there were inefficiencies in the NHS, the removal of which would ease the pressure on funding, and they resolved to use market forces (in other words, to introduce an element of price competition) to overcome these inefficiencies. For a market to work, you need providers (of goods and services) and purchasers. The purchasers need the freedom to choose between several providers, and to have extensive information about the price and quality of the goods or services offered by each provider.

Logically, therefore, the government should have given us back our taxes and left us free to shop around for the best deals. We could have

chosen the hospital that offered us the cheapest hip replacement operation and kept the change. Of course, that isn't what they did; governments give back taxes as willingly as water flows uphill and, anyway,
there is a significant section of the population that pays no tax. Instead,
they asked the district health authorities (DHAs) and the GPs to act as
purchasers on our behalf and, by doing so, they began to water down
the principle of the market and, arguably, its benefits.

The scheme was designed to work as follows.

Hospital trusts

Before the reforms, hospitals were operated and funded by DHAs. The
government wanted the DHAs, and later the GPs, to become 'purchasers' and the hospitals to become 'providers' in the new health market-
place. Hospitals (or groups of hospitals) were told to form themselves
into NHS trusts, which would act as independent businesses but with a
number of crucial (and market-diluting) differences. They were to calcu-
late the cost of all the treatment they offered and to price it at cost to
the GP purchasers. In addition, and on the assumption that there were
inefficiencies within the system that needed rooting out, they were told
to reduce this cost by 3% annually.

GP fundholders

GPs were encouraged to become 'fundholders'. Historically, GPs have
received money according to a formula based largely on the number and
age of the patients registered with them. In addition, they were now to
receive annually a sum of money (the fund) based on the cost of hospital treatment and prescribed drugs received by their patients. They were
to be empowered to buy hospital treatment for their patients at the best
price they could find. If they could do this at a total cost lower than the
fund, they could invest the surplus in their 'practice' for the benefit of
their patients. (The fundholding scheme was not designed to cover the
cost of acute emergency work.)

Hospitals

The effect of the reforms was dramatic and largely unpopular. Particularly unpopular was the assertion that old hospitals in areas of low
population density were not economically viable and should be closed.
St Bartholomew's Hospital in the City of London was an example.
Suddenly there were winners and losers in a world that had considered
itself removed from the pressures of commercial life.

The 1997 reforms

The Government White Paper of 1997 (entitled 'The New NHS: Modern,
Dependable') made a number of suggestions.

- The replacement of the internal market with 'integrated care'. This
  involved the formation of 500 Primary Care Groups typically covering

100,000 patients – bringing together family doctors and community nurses – replacing GP fundholding, which ceased to exist in 1999.

- NHSnet. Every GP surgery and hospital would be connected via the internet – it would mean less waiting for prescriptions, quicker appointments and less delay in getting results of tests.
- New services for patients. Everyone with suspected cancer would be guaranteed an appointment with a specialist within two weeks.
- NHS Direct. A 24-hour nurse-led telephone advice and information service.
- Savings. £1 billion savings from cutting paperwork would be ploughed back into patient care.

Rationing

Any suggestion of 'rationing' healthcare causes the public great concern.

The issue hit the headlines in January 1999 when Frank Dobson (then Health Secretary) announced that, because of lack of funds, the use of Viagra (an anti-impotence drug) would be rationed: the NHS would only provide Viagra for cases of impotence arising from a small number of named causes. For example, a man whose impotence was caused by diabetes could be prescribed Viagra on the NHS, whereas if the cause was kidney failure, he would have to pay for the drug privately. The publicity surrounding Viagra alerted people to other issues, in particular rationing by age and postcode prescribing.

Rationing by age

The charity Age Concern commissioned a Gallup poll that, it claimed, revealed that older people were being denied healthcare and being poorly treated in both primary and secondary care. The BMA responded by arguing that people of different ages require different patterns of treatment or referral. They cited the example of the progression of cancer, which is more rapid in younger people and often needs more aggressive radiotherapy, chemotherapy or surgery.

Postcode prescribing

Until the formation of the National Institute for Clinical Excellence (NICE) (see below) in 1999, health authorities received little guidance on what drugs and treatments to prescribe. Some well-publicised cases revealed large differences in the range of drugs and treatments available between regions (hence the term 'postcode rationing'). Beta interferon, a drug that extends the remission from multiple sclerosis (MS) in some patients, was prescribed by some health authorities but not by others, and the press highlighted cases where patients were forced to pay thousands of pounds a year to buy the drug privately, when others at an identical stage of MS, but who lived a few miles away, received the drug on the NHS.

Another well-publicised issue is that of infertility treatment (IVF). Whether or not treatment on the NHS is provided depends very much on which part of the country you live in. Across the country, about one in five infertile couples receive IVF treatment (although this figure is much higher in some areas). In February 2004 the government announced that the target is to rise to 4 in 5, and that the provision will be uniform across the country. Although this may sound very encouraging to prospective parents, there is (of course!) a downside: at the moment, infertile couples who are eligible for IVF receive up to three sets of treatment, giving a one in two chance of conception. Under the new arrangements, couples will have only one set of treatment, reducing the chances of conception to one in four. After that, they have to pay for the treatment themselves.

NICE

The National Institute for Clinical Excellence (NICE) was set up as a Special Health Authority in April 1999. In April 2005 it merged with the Health Development Agency to become the new National Institute for Health and Clinical Excellence, which is still known as NICE. Its role is to provide the NHS with guidance on individual health technologies (for instance, drugs) and treatments. In the words of the Chairman of NICE, Professor Sir Michael Rawlins, '*NICE is about taking a look at what's available, identifying what works and helping the NHS to get more of what works into practice*'. The government has acknowledged that there are variations in the quality of care available to different patients in different parts of the country, and it hopes that the guidance that NICE can provide will reduce these differences.

In a speech explaining the role of NICE, the Chairman said that it has been estimated that, on average, health professionals should be reading 19 medical and scientific articles each day if they are to keep up to date – in future, they can read the NICE bulletins instead.

It is unlikely, however, that NICE will end the controversies surrounding new treatments, since it will be making recommendations based not only on clinical effectiveness but also on cost-effectiveness – something that is very difficult to judge. A good example of a situation where a drug can be clinically effective but not cost-effective is the case of the first drug that NICE reviewed as a new treatment for influenza, called zanamivir (Relenza). Despite a hefty publicity campaign when it was introduced, NICE advised doctors and health authorities not to prescribe the drug. NICE argued that although the clinical trials showed that, if taken within 48 hours of the onset of symptoms, the duration of flu is reduced by 24 hours, there was no evidence that it would prevent the 3,000 to 4,000 deaths a year that result from complications from flu.

In addition to Relenza, NICE has investigated the effectiveness of many treatments, including:

- hip replacement joints
- therapy for depression

- treatments for Crohn's disease
- IVF treatment (see above)
- drugs for hepatitis C
- surgery for colorectal cancer
- drugs for breast cancer (taxanes)
- drugs for brain cancer (temozolomides)
- identification and management of eating disorders such as anorexia nervosa
- laser treatment in eye surgery
- treatments for obesity
- coronary artery stents.

Full details of the results of these and other investigations can be found on the NICE website (www.nice.org.uk).

2004 reforms: foundation hospitals

'What will they ask me about the NHS?' is a common question from students about to attend medical school interviews. Judging by recent feedback, the most popular topic is foundation hospitals, the government's latest reform of the NHS. NHS Foundation Trusts, to give them their proper title, are being established to provide greater ownership and involvement of patients in their local hospitals. A board of governors is elected locally and has a large say in the running of the hospitals. Direct elections for the board of governors should (it is hoped) ensure that services are directed more closely at the local community. Hospitals have been allowed to apply for Foundation Trust status since April 2004. There are now 52 Foundation Trusts.

If you listen to the news or read the newspapers, you will be aware that not everyone is happy with the idea of Foundation Trusts. Critics argue that a 'two-tier' NHS will result, with the rich and powerful Foundation Trusts able to offer higher pay to staff at the expense of other (less wealthy) hospitals. There are also concerns that Foundation Trusts will treat too many private patients in order to increase income. This, say critics, will be an inevitable outcome of a system where Foundation Trusts can borrow money from the government to improve services and facilities. First drafts of the government's bill referred to Foundation Trusts as 'companies', raising fears of the privatisation of the NHS.

2006 reforms: patient choice

You might also be asked about the recent NHS reforms relating to patient choice and payment by results, both of which came into force in the first half of 2006. Patients are now able to choose the hospital that will treat them for non-emergency cases from a list of four or more. The government is also introducing a new funding system in which hospitals are paid per patient treated, and more private hospitals will be paid by the NHS for operations on NHS patients. More information on these reforms is available at www.dh.gov.uk/en/Managingyourorganisation/Healthreform/index.htm, and a good overview of the issues surrounding patient choice can be found at http://news.bbc.co.uk/1/hi/health/ 4746573.stm.

Figure 3 shows the current structure of the NHS and the four main bodies.

2009 reforms: NHS National Quality Programme

Building on the previous decade of reforms the government is hoping to implement the above scheme to put into effect 'quality control mechanisms'. The Government has asserted that the NHS aspires to be a 'world class' health system.

This will involve:

- developing a coherent and integrated approach to improving quality
- the formation of a national Quality Steering Group which will identify priorities and resources to improve the nation's health and develop further excellent clinical leadership and professionalism.

For more on this go to: Department of Health and search under National Quality Board www.dh.gov.uk/en/Healthcare/Highqualitycareforall/NationalQualityBoard/index.htm

Current organisation and structure

These are:

- Strategic Health Authorities (SHA): in charge of planning the health care for their regions

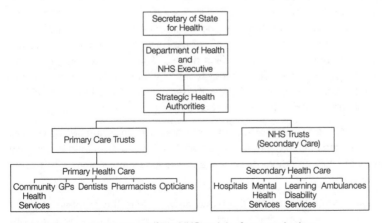

Figure 3 The current structure of the NHS and the four main bodies

- Primary Care Trusts (PCT): provide the primary care services, such as GPs, dentists, pharmacists and district nurses
- NHS Trusts: provide secondary care (including hospitals and ambulances)
- Special Health Authorities: provide services nationally, such as the National Blood Authority and NICE.

NHS spending

- Chancellor Alistair Darling announced a 4% a year rise for the NHS for three years – from £90 billion in 2009 to £110 billion in 2010.
- In the past five years, the NHS's spending on drugs has increased by almost 50% to £8 billion.
- Much of the increase in NHS funding has been spent on the workforce. GP and consultant pay is now among the highest in Europe, and it is estimated that about 40% of the £4.5 billion extra allocated to the NHS for 2006/07 will be spent on pay rises for NHS staff.
- The NHS employs 300,000 more staff now than it did in 1996. This has had the effect of reducing waiting lists and waiting times significantly (at least on paper).

After the NHS, a second area of issues is on some of the illnesses and lifestyle diseases that are topical in the media. Thus an awareness and knowledge of the following will save you some embarrassment when you are asked to comment on swine flu and/or major pandemics such as AIDS.

■ Swine flu

As with the 'bird flu' scare in 2005 and 2006, the medical headlines in 2009 have been dominated by the 'swine flu' (H1N1) pandemic. To date, since the virus was first identified in April 2009, there have been nearly 9,000 deaths attributed to it worldwide, spread across over 200 countries. Estimates of the number of people being affected by the condition vary from between 1 and 4 million people. The estimates vary because the symptoms are similar to other types of influenza, and because some countries have stopped counting milder cases. In the UK, around 300 people are reported to have died as a direct result of the virus.

The H1N1 is a new virus, containing genes from a number of viruses (human and animal), and so more people were affected than is normally the case for 'seasonal flu' since there is less natural immunity to this new virus.

Governments throughout the world have tackled the problem in different ways – Mexico, for example, closed public buildings. Many countries embarked on a programme of vaccinations targeting the 'at risk' groups: pregnant women, young children, and patients with respiratory and other problems.

The vaccines contain either live or dead viruses, and are administered either through injections or nasally. Antiviral drugs (zanamivir and oseltamivir) are used to treat patients who have contracted the illness.

The H1N1 pandemic has raised a number of questions (some of which have been discussed in recent medical school interviews).

- Demand for the vaccine outstrips supplies in many countries, which means that governments have to decide how, and to whom, they are made available. In some countries, there is an increasingly active black market trade in the vaccine, meaning that those who can afford it and who are willing to buy it directly are able to get the vaccine, whereas poorer people cannot.
- Many governments (including the UK) launched large-scale publicity campaigns soon after H1N1 was identified as being a threat, raising (some might argue) unnecessary concerns amongst the population, which in turn put extra pressures on already-stretched health service resources.
- Public reaction to the condition was arguably more extreme, given that the virus was publicised as being 'swine flu' rather than H1N1 or another seasonal flu. The same happened with 'bird flu' two years earlier.

For current information, visit the WHO's Global Alert and Responses pages at www.who.int/csr/.

MRSA and *C. difficile*

Ten years ago, most people had not heard of methicillin-resistant *Staphylococcus aureus* (MRSA). Now, horror stories abound (not all of them true) of people going into hospital to have an in-growing toenail treated, and having to stay for six months due to picking up an MRSA infection while there. It is estimated that 100,000 people each year catch the infection in UK hospitals, and that 5,000 of them die from it. The true extent of the problem is not really known. Government statistics show an official figure (that is, with MRSA recorded on the death certificate) of about 1,200 deaths from MRSA in 2008, a fall of 23% compared to the previous year. This is not to say that there is any form of cover-up; it is simply that many people who are infected with MRSA in hospitals die from causes associated with the conditions that caused them to be in hospital in the first place.

The rate of infection in the UK is one of the highest in the world because of poor hygiene in hospitals. The infection spreads via staff who handle different patients throughout the day without washing their hands in between contact with one patient and the next, or because hospital wards are not cleaned properly. If the organisms that cause MRSA get into the blood system of people weakened by illness or age, through a wound or an injection, the effects can be very serious. Since the organism is resistant to many antibiotics, it is extremely difficult to treat.

In December 2004, the *Independent* reported that the NHS spends more than £1 billion a year in trying to prevent and treat the disease, and that over the previous seven years the number of deaths from MRSA had doubled.

There were around 2,500 deaths attributed to *Clostridium difficile* (*C. difficile*), another hospital-acquired infection, reported in 2008, a 29% decrease over 2007.

Some issues that have been brought up in interviews recently:

- Why are there not accurate figures about the numbers of deaths caused by MRSA and *C. difficile*?
- What is being done to try to prevent infections?
- Why might the organisms be resistant to antibiotics?
- Why are death rates now falling?

UK health

It would be a good idea to do a little bit of research on the 'lifestyle' diseases listed in Table 3, which are the big killers in Western countries.

Table 3 Primary lifestyle diseases in Western countries

Cause of death	Male	Female
All	240,000	270,000
Infectious diseases	2,700	3,500
Ischaemic heart disease	49,000	39,000
Respiratory disease	33,000	40,000
Cancer (all)	72,000	67,000
Cancer (respiratory system)	18,000	12,000
Cancer (digestive system)	21,000	17,000
Cancer (breast)	80	11,000
Cancer (secondary)	5,500	6,500
Cancer (colon)	4,500	4,500
Cancer (prostate)	9,000	0
Cancer (skin)	1,100	1000

Source: UK Statistics Authority (www.statistics.gov.uk)

In an interview you should be able to discuss possible reasons for the changes in death rates from causes such as cancer and heart problems, and for the difference in mortality rates between men and women.

A third area that may generate questions in interviews is the state of medicine and healthcare in less economically developed countries (LEDCs). The nature of diseases and causes of death in poor countries are very different from those of the West.

Therefore, an understanding of the major water-borne diseases, like cholera, and contagious diseases such as smallpox and/or leprosy is of value. In addition, many of these countries have the extra burden that comes with improving incomes and life expectancies: the number of lifestyle diseases, such as cancer, is on the increase.

World health: rich v. poor

The world population is about 6.8 billion and growing. The biggest killers are infectious diseases (25 million since 1981) such as AIDS, malaria and tuberculosis, and circulatory diseases (17 million) such as coronary heart disease and stroke. Cancer killed about 7 million people.

Infectious diseases that were once thought to be under control, such as tuberculosis, cholera and yellow fever, have made a comeback. This is due, in part, to the increasing resistance of certain bacteria to antibiotics. The antibiotics that we use now are essentially modifications to drugs that have been in use for the past 30 or 40 years, and random genetic mutations allow resistant strains to multiply.

The effects of an ageing population

Life expectancy continues to rise (except in many sub-Saharan African countries, which have been ravaged by HIV/AIDS – see page 110) because of improvements in sanitation and medical care. According to the WHO, the number of people aged 60 or over will more than triple by 2050, from about 600 million now to 2 billion. Birth rates in most countries are falling, and the combination of the two brings considerable problems. The relative number of people who succumb to chronic illness (such as cancer, diabetes or diseases of the circulatory system) is increasing, and this puts greater strains on countries' healthcare systems. A useful indicator is the dependency ratio – the percentage of the population that is economically dependent on the active age group. It is calculated as the sum of 0- to 14-year-olds and over-65s divided by the number of people aged between 15 and 59. This is rising steadily. The WHO website contains data for each country (www.who.int).

In the industrialised world, infectious diseases are well under control. The main threats to health are circulatory diseases (such as heart disease and stroke), cancer, respiratory ailments and musculoskeletal conditions (rheumatic diseases and osteoporosis). All of these are diseases that tend to affect older people and, as life expectancy is increasing, they will become more prevalent in the future. Many are nutrition related, where an unhealthy diet rich in saturated fats and processed foods leads to poor health. In poorer countries, infectious diseases such as malaria, cholera, tuberculosis, hepatitis and HIV/AIDS are much more common. Malaria affects up to 500 million people a year and kills over a million, and 1.5 million die from tuberculosis. The UN estimated that in 2007, 2.5 million people were newly infected with HIV/AIDS and 2.1 million people died from AIDS-related causes.

Infectious diseases go hand in hand with poverty; overcrowding, lack of clean water and poor sanitation all encourage the spread of diseases, and lack of money reduces the access to drugs and treatment.

The WHO estimates that nearly 2 million deaths worldwide each year are attributable to unsafe water, and poor sanitation and hygiene.

In its report on infectious diseases published in 2000, the WHO highlighted the problem of antimicrobial resistance. Although antimicrobial resistance is a natural phenomenon, the result of genetic mutation and 'survival of the fittest', the effect has been amplified in recent years by the misuse of antimicrobials. Many treatments that were effective 10 years ago are no longer so, and it is a sobering thought that there have been no major new developments in antimicrobial drugs for 30 years. Given that new drugs take at least 10 years to develop and test, it is easy to see that a problem is looming. The WHO's former director-general, Dr Gro Harlem Brundtland, was quoted in the health pages of the CNN website (www.cnn.com/health) as saying: 'We currently have effective medicines to cure almost every infectious disease, but we risk losing these valuable drugs and our opportunity to control infectious diseases.'

Although it is commonly stated that the overuse of antimicrobials is the cause of the problem, it might be argued that it is actually the underuse that has done the damage, since it is the pathogens that survive that cause the resistance.

Tourism also plays a part in the spread of diseases. The number of cases of malaria, yellow fever and other infectious diseases in developed countries is increasing as tourists catch the infections prior to returning to their own countries.

Life expectancy

Life expectancy figures for selected countries are shown in Table 4.

These figures could be the source of many interview questions.

- Why does Japan have the highest life expectancy?
- Why does France have a higher life expectancy than the UK?

Table 4 Life expectancy figures for selected countries

Country	Life expectancy
Japan	81.9
France	79.8
UK	78.2
USA	77.3
Afghanistan	42.6
Angola	39.9
Zimbabwe	37.9
Lesotho	35.7

Source: World Health Organisation (www.who.int)

■   Why is the healthy life expectancy (HALE) in Afghanistan low?
■   Why are most of the countries with the lowest HALE figures located in the middle and southern parts of Africa?

You can probably guess the answers to these, but if not, a discussion of these questions can be found at www.mpw.co.uk/getintomed, and further data is available at www3.who.int/whosis/core/core_select. cfm. Table 5 also provides some ideas.

Healthcare expenditure

Table 5 shows the 2007 and 2005 figures respectively for per capita government expenditure on health in US dollars and total health expenditure as a percentage of GDP.

Table 5 Per capita government expenditure on health and total health expenditure as a percentage of GDP (2007 and 2005)

Country	Per capita expenditure on health (2007, US$)*	Total health expenditure as a percentage of GDP (2005, £)†
Japan	2293	8.2
UK	2501	8.1
Luxembourg	5178	7.7
India	5	5.0
Zimbabwe	12	7.5
Mozambique	42	4.3

* Source: United Nations Human Development Report 2007 (http://hdr.undp.org)
† Source: World Health Organization (www.who.int)

■ HIV/AIDS

To date, about 70 million people have become infected since the disease was first recognised in 1981, and 30 million have died. The number of new infections and deaths is slowing down globally as a result of improved education and the wider availability of treatments. The number of people with HIV who received antiretroviral (ARV) treatment in 2008 was about 4 million (although the WHO estimates that there are a further 9.5 million people who require ARV therapy). In the worst affected continent, Africa, there is a decline in the number of new infections of up to 25% in six countries within the 15 to 24 age group. This goes hand in hand with a decline in the rate of sex among young people and the increased use of condoms. However, in some parts of the world, such as Eastern Europe and Central Asia, the number of new infections continues to rise. In contrast, the number of people living with HIV/AIDS is increasing, thanks to the effectiveness of antiretroviral therapies.

Table 6 shows regional statistics for HIV and AIDS for 2008. These statistics on the world epidemic of AIDS and HIV have been published by UNAIDS/WHO in December 2009.

Some of you might have noticed that the figures in this table are significantly different from the previous year's figures. This is because the WHO has revised its estimates after adopting improved information collecting and surveillance methods. The WHO's current estimate of about

Table 6 Regional statistics for HIV and AIDS for 2008

Region	Adults and children living with HIV/AIDS	Adults and children newly infected	Adult prevalence*	Deaths of adults and children
Sub-Saharan Africa	22.4 million	1.9 million	5.2%	1.4 million
North Africa and Middle East	310,000	35,000	0.2%	20,000
Asia	4.65 million	350,000	0.2%	330,000
Oceania	59,000	3,900	0.3%	2,000
Latin America	2 million	170,000	0.6%	77,000
Caribbean	240,000	20,000	1.0%	12,000
Eastern Europe and Central Asia	1.5 million	110,000	0.7%	87,000
North America, Western and Central Europe	2.25 million	85,000	0.4%	36,000
Global total	33.4 million	2.7 million	0.8%	2.0 million

Source: World Health Organization AIDS Epidemic Update December 2009
* Proportion of adults aged 15–49 who were living with HIV/AIDS.

33 million people living with HIV replaces the 2006 estimate of nearly 40 million. It is estimated that only one in 10 of the people who are infected with HIV or AIDS is aware of the fact. In regions where ARV therapy is freely available, there is a significant increase in the number of people who are prepared to undergo HIV/AIDS testing. This has the effect of raising awareness, which in turn reduces the stigma and encourages people to discuss and to confront the disease. This is an important factor in reducing the rate of infection.

It is clear that the only effective way of tackling HIV/AIDS is to adopt sustained and comprehensive programmes in affected areas; short-term measures or individual charities working in isolation have little chance of making a significant impact. The WHO has identified some of the elements that are important in an AIDS/HIV programme:

- availability of cheap (or free) male and female condoms
- availability of free ARV therapy
- availability of effective and free treatment of all sexually transmitted diseases
- education programmes
- clear policies on human rights and effective antidiscrimination legislation
- willingness on the part of national governments to take the lead in the programme.

Currently there are 21 vaccines undergoing trials.

Women and AIDS

In some sub-Saharan African countries more than 75% of young people living with HIV/AIDS are women, and in the sub-Saharan region as a whole the rate of infection among women in the 15 to 24 age group is over three times greater than that among males in the same age group. Yet surveys in parts of Zimbabwe and South Africa indicate that nearly 70% of women have only ever had one sexual partner, and education programmes targeting women have been relatively effective. The main cause of the spread of the infection in Africa (and increasingly in India and South-East Asia) is through men having unprotected sex with sex workers and subsequently passing on the disease to their partners. This, in turn, increases the incidences of mother-to-baby infection.

Natural disasters

In the past 18 months the landslides and floods in Brazil and the earthquake in Haiti have tended to focus the world's attention on the devastation caused by a natural disaster, particularly if it is in the less developed world. However, don't forget that developed nations are also affected, for example the Australian bushfires last year and the Italian earthquake. Whenever a natural disaster occurs (floods, earthquakes or other events that displace people from their homes), food supplies are affected and clean water supplies are contaminated, which results in an enormous increase in infectious diseases such as diarrhoea, cholera and typhoid. In addition, malnutrition and difficulties in providing adequate medical treatment contribute to the number of deaths. Obviously though, Western nations can cope with these emergencies much better than poor ones.

The earthquake in Pakistan in October 2005 killed 73,000 people, left another 70,000 injured and made 3 million homeless. As well as the problems associated with a lack of clean drinking water, it is estimated that in the three months following the earthquake, 13,000 women delivered babies and many of these mothers and their children needed immediate medical attention.

Even the world's richest and most powerful country, the US, was unable to cope with the aftermath of Hurricane Katrina, which hit the Gulf of Mexico in August 2005 and killed over 1,300 people, leaving a further 375,000 homeless. Man-made disasters, particularly wars and persecution of ethnic groups, also cause people to be displaced from their homes, and many of the same problems caused by natural disasters are prevalent.

Lastly, a very relevant and current area that has caused large amounts of discussion and, indeed, can often polarise opinions is the weighted and complex questions that have a moral and/or ethical dimension. Many medical students with whom I have spoken tell me that, almost without exception, either one or several of the following issues were discussed at the interview stage.

Genes: medical and ethical issues

Many illnesses are thought to be caused by defective genes: examples are cancer, cystic fibrosis and Alzheimer's disease. The defects may be hereditary or can be triggered by external factors such as ionising or solar radiation. The much-hyped dream of medical researchers, especially in the US, is that the affected chromosomes could be repaired, allowing the body to heal itself.

To make this dream come true, scientists need to discover which gene is causing the problem and work out how to replace it with a healthy one. Great progress has been made in solving the first part of the puzzle, thanks to a gigantic international research project known as the Human Genome Project, which has as its aim the identification of every human gene and an understanding of what effect it has. The full sequence was published in early 2000. Many links have been made between diseases and specific genes, but the techniques for replacing the defective genes have yet to prove themselves.

Two methods have been proposed.

1| The healthy gene is incorporated into a retro-virus which, by its nature, splices its genetic material into the chromosomes of the host cell. The virus must first be treated in order to prevent it causing problems of its own. This 'denaturing' reduces the positive effects and, to date, the trials have been unconvincing.

2| The healthy gene is incorporated into a fatty droplet, which is sprayed into the nose in order to reach cells in the lining of the nose, air passages and lungs, or injected into the blood. It was hoped that this method would be effective against the single defective gene that causes cystic fibrosis but, again, the trials have yet to prove successful.

To make matters more complicated, it turns out that many of the illnesses that are genetic in origin are caused by defects in a wide number of genes, so the hoped-for magic bullet needs to be replaced by a magic cluster bomb – and that sounds suspiciously like the approach used by conventional pharmaceuticals. Since 1990, when gene therapy for humans began, about 300 clinical trials (involving diseases ranging from cystic fibrosis and heart disease to brain tumours) have been carried out, with very limited success.

Genetic engineering

Genetic engineering is the name given to the manipulation of genes. There is a subtle difference between genetic engineering and gene therapy: specifically, that genetic engineering implies modification of the genes involved in reproduction. These modifications will then be carried over into future generations.

One of the reasons for considering these ideas is to try to produce enhanced performance in animals and plants. The possibility of applying genetic engineering to humans poses major ethical problems and, at present, experiments involving reproductive cells are prohibited. Nevertheless, one form of genetic engineering known as genetic screening is allowed. In this technique, an egg is fertilised in a test tube. When the embryo is two days old, one cell is removed and the chromosomes are tested to establish the sex and presence of gene defects. In the light of the tests, the parents decide whether or not to implant the embryo into the mother's womb.

Taken to its logical conclusion, this is the recipe for creating a breed of supermen. The superman concept may be morally acceptable when applied to race horses, but should it be applied to merchant bankers?

How would we feel if a small, undemocratic state decided to apply this strategy to its entire population in order to obtain an economic advantage? Could we afford to ignore this challenge?

The fundamental argument against any policy that reduces variation in the human gene pool is that it is intrinsically dangerous because, in principle, it restricts the species' ability to adapt to new environmental challenges. Inability to adapt to an extreme challenge could lead to the extinction of our species.

Human cloning

The breakthrough in cloning technology came in 1997 in the form of Dolly the sheep – see page 115. In February 2004, a group of South Korean scientists led by Dr Hwang announced that it had succeeded in cloning 30 human embryos to obtain stem cells, which could one day be used to treat diseases. Stem cells can develop into any type of cell in the human body and could be used to repair or replace damaged organs. They followed up this announcement in May 2005 by claiming that they had extracted cells from the cloned embryos that matched exactly the cells of 11 patients.

However, in December 2005, Seoul National University (where Dr Hwang and his team worked) concluded that the results were fabricated. Dr Hwang subsequently resigned, while maintaining that the scientific basis for his claims was still valid and that Korea led the world in stem cell research.

There have been many claims in the past for the successful cloning of a human embryo. A number of doctors announced that they were either working on, or had successfully performed, human cloning. Names that may have come to your attention include an American, Dr Richard Seed; Dr Severino Antinori; Dr Panos Zavos (whose claim to have created the world's first cloned human embryo has yet to be substantiated); and an organisation called Clonaid, founded by a religious cult.

It is important to make the distinction between reproductive cloning – the reproduction of genetically identical individuals – and therapeutic cloning, which does not involve the creation of genetically identical people but uses the same techniques to produce replacement organs or to repair damaged organs.

The BMA 'considers unacceptable the notion of cloning whole humans and would not wish to see public policy develop in this way', but would like to see 'rational debate about the subject in order to ensure that public policies in this sphere can be supported by the strength of argument, and not solely by the strength of opinion'.

Therapeutic cloning could be used to produce embryonic stem cells, which could then develop into specific types of tissue to repair or replace damaged organs. It is thought that stem cells could be used, for example, in the treatment of Parkinson's disease, to provide bone marrow for leukaemia treatment, to repair damaged heart muscles and to produce new skin for burns victims.

The BMA supports research into therapeutic cloning, '*including research using human embryos where necessary for the development of tissue for transplantation; and the development of methods of therapy for mitochondrial diseases*'. In August 2004, scientists at the Newcastle NHS Fertility Centre were given a licence to create Europe's first cloned human embryos for research. See the BBC website (www.bbc.co.uk) for some very good analysis of cloning issues.

Reasons why people may want human cloning:

- for those who are infertile
- to 'recover' a child who has died
- for eugenics – to improve the human race
- for spare parts
- for research purposes.

Reasons why people are against human cloning:

- health risks from mutation of genes
- risks of abuse of the technology
- ethical/religious reasons
- emotional risks for cloned child.

Dolly the sheep and the Roslin Institute

Dolly, born at the Roslin Institute in Edinburgh, hit the headlines in February 1997 because she was the first mammal to be cloned from an adult cell. The importance of the birth is not the fact that a sheep had been cloned, as this had been done before using embryo cells, but that nobody had successfully taken adult cells – in this case from the udder of a six-year-old ewe – and cloned them.

Embryo cells have the potential to become complete embryos, but adult cells are differentiated – for instance, cells in the liver do the job of the liver – and so cloning is much more difficult. The process begins by starving cells of nutrients for a few days until they stop growing and dividing. The nucleus of one of these quiescent cells is then injected into an egg cell that has previously had its nucleus removed. A small electric current is used to kick the cell back into activity, and it is then put into the womb of a female sheep to grow. The egg now contains a full set of genes, as if it had been fertilised by a spermatozoa. It took 277 attempts to produce the first successful clone.

The difference between cloning and IVF treatment is that, in the latter, eggs are fertilised in a test tube (hence the so-called 'test tube babies' phrase) using sperm from a male, and then placed in the uterus, whereas cloning involves the removal of the egg nucleus, which is then replaced by the nucleus of the cell that is to be cloned. A cloned animal has only one parent.

Cloning could be an important source of genetically identical copies of organs, skin and blood cells for surgical use. The biotechnology company PPL Therapeutics, which worked with the Roslin scientists, hopes to use the cloning technique to produce sheep capable of generating the blood-clotting protein Factor IX in their milk. PPL estimates that 50 sheep would be enough to produce the £100 million annual world demand for Factor IX. In January 2002, it was discovered that Dolly had arthritis. It is unusual for sheep under six years old to get arthritis in the rear legs, and this has raised fears that premature ageing could be a result of cloning. There is also chromosome evidence that Dolly aged faster than non-cloned sheep. If organs from cloned animals are one day going to be used for human transplants, will they age prematurely in the human's body?

On 14 February 2003, Dolly was put down at the relatively young age of six years because the scientists decided that she would not recover from a progressive lung disease. Dr Harry Griffin, the acting Director at Roslin, said, '*Sheep can live to 11 or 12 years of age, and lung diseases are common in older sheep, particularly those housed indoors.*' There is no evidence that cloning was a factor in Dolly contracting the disease. The post-mortem did not uncover any other abnormalities.

In January 2007, the Roslin Institute announced that it had bred genetically modified chickens that lay eggs that contain medicinal proteins, from which drugs can be produced. The modified genes within the chickens' DNA are passed from generation to generation. One of the breeds of chickens produces interferon, used to treat multiple sclerosis, and there are hopes that similar breeds could produce drugs that could treat arthritis and various forms of cancer.

Euthanasia and assisted deaths

Euthanasia is illegal in the UK, and doctors who are alleged to have given a patient a lethal dose of a medication with the intention of ending that person's life have been charged with murder. UK law also prohibits assisting with suicide. The Suicide Act of 1961 decriminalised suicide in England and Wales, but assisting a suicide is a crime under that legislation.

Section 2(1) Suicide Act 1961 provides:

> *A person who aids, abets, counsels or procures the suicide of another, or an attempt by another to commit suicide, shall be liable on conviction on indictment to imprisonment for a term not exceeding fourteen years.*

However, in order to prove the offence of aiding and abetting it is necessary to prove firstly, that the person in question had taken their own life and, secondly, that an individual or individuals had aided and abetted the person in committing suicide.

In December 2004, a High Court judge allowed a husband to take his wife (referred to as Mrs Z in the case) to Switzerland – where the law on euthanasia is different – to help her to die. Mrs Z was unable to travel alone as she had an incurable brain disease, but the local authorities had tried to prevent her husband taking her. It is now expected that more people in the UK will travel to Switzerland to be allowed to die. It was reported in the *Observer* in December 2004 that an estimated 3% of GPs in the UK had helped patients to die. The *Observer* also stated that in a poll of doctors, 54% favoured legalising euthanasia. The BMA website provides detailed information on the law in a number of countries, and the ethical considerations behind euthanasia. Links to this, and to other related websites, can be found on www.mpw.co.uk/getintomed.

Nevertheless the debate is ongoing and a very recent example of the conundrum that exists to date is the case of the rugby player Daniel James, who in 2007 was made a tetraplegic after a rugby accident. After several attempts at suicide in the UK he was directed to Dignitas in Switzerland, where he committed suicide in 2008.

The police have investigated the acts of Daniel's parents and a family friend and concluded that there would be sufficient evidence to prosecute each of them for an offence of aiding and abetting Daniel's suicide; contrary to the law (see above), it was decided that, on the particular facts of this case, a prosecution would not be in the public interest. It is interesting that the police are taking this stance, but it does reflect the complexity of such ethical matters. See www.cps.gov.uk/news/articles/death_by_suicide_of_daniel_james/

In another case as reported by the BBC in 2009 a woman with multiple sclerosis made legal history by winning her battle to have the law on assisted suicide clarified. Debbie Purdy wanted to know if her husband would be prosecuted if he helped her end her life in Switzerland. See http://news.bbc.co.uk/1/hi/8176713.stm. Five Law Lords ruled that the Director of Public Prosecutions (DPP) must specify when a person might face prosecution. Ms Purdy said the Law Lords' decision was '*a huge step towards a more compassionate law*'.

In February 2010 the DPP published its revised policy on prosecuting assisted suicide cases. The Crown Prosecution website gives details of the public interest factors against prosecution. These include:

1| the victim had reached a voluntary, clear, settled and informed decision to commit suicide
2| the suspect was wholly motivated by compassion

3| the actions of the suspect, although sufficient to come within the definition of the offence, were of only minor encouragement or assistance

4| the suspect had sought to dissuade the victim from taking the course of action which resulted in his or her suicide

5| the actions of the suspect may be characterised as reluctant encouragement or assistance in the face of a determined wish on the part of the victim to commit suicide

6| the suspect reported the victim's suicide to the police and fully assisted them in their enquiries into the circumstances of the suicide or the attempt and his or her part in providing encouragement or assistance.

Source: www.cps.gov.uk/publications/prosecution/ assisted_suicide_policy.html

Writing in *The Times* on the day that the new guidelines were released, Keir Starmer, Director of Public Prosecutions, stated:

Assisted suicide involves assisting the victim to take his or her own life. Someone who takes the life of another undertakes a very different act and may well be liable to a charge of murder or manslaughter. That distinction is an important one that we all need to understand.

Ultimately, as many people recognised, each case is unique; each case has to be considered on its own facts and merits; and prosecutors have to make professional judgements about difficult and sensitive issues.

The assisted suicide policy will help them in that task.

Source: www.timesonline.co.uk/tol/comment/columnists/ guest_contributors/article7039977.ece

For more information about the DPP's policy on assisted suicide, please see www.cps.gov.uk/publications/prosecution/assisted_suicide_policy. html.

■ The internet

The internet provides the medical world with many opportunities but also some problems. The wealth of medical information available on the internet enables doctors to gain access to new research, treatments and diagnostic methods quickly. Communication between doctors, hospitals, research groups and governing bodies is simple, and news (e.g. the outbreak of a disease) can be sent around the world in a matter of minutes. The internet can also be used to create web-based administrative systems, such as online appointment booking for patients.

For patients, the internet can be used to find out about treatments for minor illnesses or injuries without having to visit a doctor or a hospital. A good site to investigate is NHS Direct (www.nhsdirect.nhs.uk), which also provides patients with a search engine to locate local doctors.

Not all of the information available, however, is reliable. Anyone can set up a website and make it appear to be authoritative. Type 'cancer', for example, into Google and you will find nearly 2 billion sites or articles listed! Some of these are extremely useful, such as information sites provided by doctors, health organisations or support groups. However, there is also an enormous number of sites selling medicines or treatments (which, in the best cases, may be harmless but could also be extremely dangerous) and quack remedies. Even if the medication that is purchased is the correct one for the condition, the drugs could be fake, of inferior quality or the incorrect dosage. In many cases, side effects from one type of medication need other drugs to control them. The internet also allows patients to self-diagnose. The dangers of doing this range from attributing symptoms to something life-threatening (and then buying harmful drugs from another website) to gaining reassurance that the condition is harmless when it might actually be something very serious.

09 Further information

Courses

Medlink/medsim

Intensive residential course at Nottingham University School of Medicine, consisting of a series of lectures covering a wide range of medical subjects. There is also a casualty simulation exercise (www.medlink-uk.com).

Future Doctors

Future Doctors specialises in helping students in their preparation for the highly competitive medical school application process with dedicated interview skills, UKCAT and BMAT guidance. It hosts weekend courses at Imperial and UCL, organises work experience/mentoring programmes and has an extensive online resource dedicated to getting you into medical school. For more information see www.futuredoctors.co.uk.

Publications

Careers in medicine

A Career in Medicine, ed. Harvey White, Royal Society of Medicine Press (www.roysocmed.ac.uk)

Careers in Medicine, Dentistry and Mental Health, Judith Humphries, Kogan Page (www.kogan-page.co.uk)

The Insider's Guide to UK Medical Schools, eds Sally Girgis, Leigh Bisset, David Burke, BMJ Books (www.wiley.com)

Learning Medicine, Peter Richards, Simon Stockill, Rosalind Foster, Elizabeth Ingall, Cambridge University Press

Medicine Uncovered, Paul Greer, Trotman (www.trotman.co.uk)

Genetics

The Blind Watchmaker, Richard Dawkins, Penguin

Clone, Gina Kolata, Allen Lane/Penguin Press

Genome, Matt Ridley, Fourth Estate

The Language of the Genes, Steve Jones, Flamingo

The Sequence, Kevin Davies, Weidenfeld and Nicolson

The Single Helix, Steve Jones, Little Brown

Who's Afraid of Human Cloning? Gregory E. Pearce, Rowman and Littlefield

Y: The Descent of Man, Steve Jones, Bantam

Higher education entry

BMAT: Preparation for the BMAT, Heinemann

Degree Course Offers, Brian Heap, Trotman

Getting into Oxford & Cambridge, MPW Guides/Trotman

How to Complete Your UCAS Application, MPW Guides/Trotman

University and College Entrance: The Official Guide, UCAS

Medical science: general

Aspirin, Diarmuid Jeffreys, Bloomsbury

Body Story, Dr David Willham, Channel 4 Books

Catching Cold, Pete Davies, Michael Joseph/Penguin

Don't Die Young, Dr Alice Roberts, Bloomsbury

Everything You Need to Know About Bird Flu, Jo Revill, Rodale

Flu, Gina Kolata, Pan

The Greatest Benefit to Mankind, Roy Porter, Fontana

How We Live, Sherwin Nuland, Vintage

The Human Brain: A Guided Tour, Susan Greenfield, Weidenfeld and Nicolson

Human Instinct, Robert Winston, Bantam

Medicine: A History of Healing, ed. Roy Porter, Michael O'Mara Books

Medicine and Culture, Lynn Payer, Victor Gollancz

The Noonday Demon: An Anatomy of Depression, Andrew Solomon, Vintage

The Oxford Companion to the Body, Blakemore and Jennett, Oxford University Press

The Oxford Illustrated Companion to Medicine, eds Stephen Lock, John M. Last and George Dunea, Oxford University Press

Pain: The Science of Suffering, Patrick Wall, Weidenfeld and Nicolson

Penicillin Man: Alexander Fleming and the Antibiotic Revolution, Kevin Brown, Sutton Publishing

Plague, Pox and Pestilence: Disease in History, Kenneth Kiple, Weidenfeld and Nicolson

Poison Arrows, Stanley Feldman, Metro

Practical Medical Ethics, David Seedhouse and Lisetta Lovett, John Wiley

The Secret Family, David Bodanis, Simon and Schuster

Stop the 21st Century Killing You, Dr Paula Baillie-Hamilton, Vermillion

The Trouble with Medicine, Dr Melvin Konner, BBC Worldwide Ltd

User's Guide to the Brain, John Ratey, Abacus

The White Death: A History of Tuberculosis, Thomas Dormandy, Hambledon

Why We Age, Steven N. Austab, John Wiley

Medical ethics

The Body Hunters, Sonia Shah, The New Press

Causing Death and Saving Lives, Jonathan Glover, Penguin

Medical practice

A Damn Bad Business: The NHS Deformed, Jeremy Lee, Victor Gollancz

Bedside Stories: Confessions of a Junior Doctor, Michael Foxton, Guardian Books

Medic One On Scene, Dr Heather Clark, Virgin

NHS Plc, Allyson M. Pollock, Verso

Patient: The True Story of a Rare Illness, Ben Watt, Viking

Patients' Choice, David Cook, Hodder and Stoughton

Repeat Prescription: Further Tales of a Rural GP, Dr Michael Sparrow, Robinson

■ Websites

All the medical schools have their own website (see below) and there are numerous useful and interesting medical sites. These can be found using search engines. Particularly informative sites include:

- Admissions forum: www.admissionsforum.net (essential information for applicants)
- BMAT: www.bmat.org.uk
- British Medical Association: www.bma.org.uk
- Department of Health: www.dh.gov.uk
- General Medical Council: www.gmc-uk.org
- Student BMJ: www.student.bmj.com
- UKCAT: www.ukcat.ac.uk
- World Health Organization: www.who.int

■ Financial advice

For information on the financial side of five to six years at medical school, see www.money4medstudents.org. This website has been prepared by the Royal Medical Benevolent Fund, in partnership with the BMA Medical Students Committee, the Council of Heads of Medical Schools and the National Association of Student Money Advisers.

■ Examiners' reports

The examining boards provide detailed reports on recent exam papers, including mark schemes and specimen answers. Schools are sent these every year by the boards. They are useful when analysing your performance in tests and mock examinations. If your school does not have copies, they can be obtained from the boards themselves. The examining boards' website addresses are:

- www.aqa.org.uk
- www.edexcel.org.uk
- www.ocr.org.uk
- www.wjec.co.uk

■ Contact details

Studying in the UK

Aberdeen
Medical Admissions
School of Medicine and Dentistry
University of Aberdeen

3rd Floor Polwarth Building
Forester Hill
Aberdeen AB25 2ZD
Tel: 01224 554975
Email: medadm@abdn.ac.uk
Web: www.abdn.ac.uk/medicine-dentistry

Birmingham
Professor Chris Lote
Medicine Admissions Tutor
Professor of Experimental Nephrology
Medical School
University of Birmingham
Birmingham B15 2TT
Tel: 0121 414 6921
Email: c.j.lote@bham.ac.uk
Web: www.medicine.bham.ac.uk

University of Brighton and Sussex Medical School
Holly Huth, Senior Admissions Officer (h.k.huth@brighton.ac.uk) Or
Brighton and Sussex Medical School
BSMS Teaching Building
University of Sussex
Brighton BN1 9PX
Tel: 01273 641966
Web: www.bsms.ac.uk

Bristol
Matthew Holt
Admissions Officer
Faculty of Medicine
University of Bristol
Senate House
Tyndall Avenue
Bristol BS8 1TH
Email: Matthew.Holt@bristol.ac.uk
Web: www.medici.bris.ac.uk

Cambridge
Tricia Smoothy
University of Cambridge
School of Clinical Medicine
Addenbrookes Hospital
Cambridge CB2 0SP
Also contact Sarah Hannaford
Email: Sarah.Hannaford@admin.cam.ac.uk
Web: www.medschl.cam.ac.uk

Cardiff

Admissions Officer
Medical School Office
Wales College of Medicine, Biology, Life and Health Sciences
Cardiff University
Heath Park Campus
Cardiff CF14 4XN
Web: www.cardiff.ac.uk/medicine

Dundee

Gordon Black, BSc, MEd
Admissions and Student Recruitment
University of Dundee
Dundee DD1 4HN
Tel: 0138 238 4032/6647
Email: g.g.black@dundee.ac.uk
Web: www.dundee.ac.uk/medicalschool

Durham

Admissions Office
Queen's Campus Stockton
University Boulevard
Stockton on Tees TS17 6BH
Email: Helen.taylor3@durham.ac.uk
Web: www.dur.ac.uk/phase1.medicine/welcome.htm
Note: Durham is exactly the same as Newcastle, which sets Durham's criteria and receives all the applications, though interviews do take place at Durham.

East Anglia

Dr D. J. Heylings
Admissions Tutor/ Senior Lecturer in Anatomy
School of Medicine, Health Policy & Practice
University of East Anglia
Norwich NR4 7TJ
Tel: 01603 593939
Email: D.Heylings@uea.ac.uk
Web: www.med.uea.ac.uk

Edinburgh

Ginny Allan
Admissions Officer
MBChB Admissions
Room SU.218
College of Medicine and Veterinary Medicine
The University of Edinburgh
The Chancellor's Building

49 Little France Crescent
Edinburgh EH16 4SB
Tel: 0131 242 6405
Email: ginny.allan@ed.ac.uk
Web: www.mvm.ed.ac.uk

Glasgow
Coleen Doherty
Admissions Administrator
Room 337
Wolfson Medical School Building
University of Glasgow
Glasgow G12 8QQ
Tel: 0141 330 6216
Email: admissions@clinmed.gla.ac.uk
Web: www.gla.ac.uk/faculties/medicine/index.html

Hull York
Julia Fletcher
Hull York Medical School
York University
Heslington
York YO10 5DD
Email: Julia.Fletcher@hyms.ac.uk
Web: www.hyms.ac.uk

Imperial College
David Gibbon
Admissions Officer
School of Medicine
Imperial College of Science, Technology and Medicine
London SW7 2AZ
Web: www.ic.ac.uk/medicine

Keele
Julia Molyneux
Admissions Administrator
School of Medicine
Keele University ST5 5BG
Web: www.keele.ac.uk/depts/ms

King's College London
Carys Barbour
Admissions Assistant
Student Admissions Office
King's College London
Hodgkin Building
Guy's Campus

London SE1 1UL
Tel: 020 7848 6501
Email: guysadmissions@kcl.ac.uk
Web: www.kcl.ac.uk/depsta/medicine

Leeds
Ann Gaunt
Admissions & Electives Administrator, Learning and Teaching
School of Medicine, Room 7.09
Level 7, Worsley Building
University of Leeds
Leeds LS2 9JT
Tel: 0113 343 4362
Email: A.E.Gaunt@leeds.ac.uk
Web: www.leeds.ac.uk/medhealth

Leicester
Anne Peppitt
Assistant Registrar
Medical School Office
University of Leicester
PO Box 138
University Road
Leicester LE1 9HN
Tel: 0116 252 2963
Email: aep5@le.ac.uk
Web: www.le.ac.uk/sm/le

Liverpool
Joanne Henderson
Admissions Officer
Cedar House
Ashton Street
Liverpool L69 3GA
Email: mbchb@liverpool.ac.uk
Web: www.liv.ac.uk/sme
Note: Lancaster University has an affiliated programme with Liverpool.
Candidates need to use L41 institution code (Liverpool) but A105 as a
course code. The entry criteria will be the same, and the point of contact will be Dr Karen Grant at Lancaster University.

Manchester
Mrs Linda Harding
Admissions Co-ordinator or
Vicky MacEwan
The Medical School
Faculty of Medical and Human Sciences
Stopford Building

University of Manchester
Oxford Road
Manchester M13 9PT
Tel: 0161 275 7556
Email: linda.m.harding@manchester.ac.uk or
vicky.macewan@manchester.ac.uk
Web: www.medicine.manchester.ac.uk

Newcastle
D. Smith
Admissions Officer
The Medical School
University of Newcastle
Framlington Place
Newcastle upon Tyne NE2 4HH
Web: http://medical.faculty.ncl.ac.uk

Nottingham
Mrs Martine Lowes
Medical Course Officer
Medical School
University of Nottingham
Queen's Medical Centre
Nottingham NG7 2UH
Tel: 0115 823 0007
Martine.Lowes@nottingham.ac.uk
Web: www.nottingham.ac.uk/mhs

Oxford
Lesley Maitland
Graduate Entry Medicine
Medical Sciences Teaching Centre
South Parks Road
Oxford OX1 3RE
Email: lesley.maitland@medsci.ox.ac.uk
Web: www.medsci.ox.ac.uk

Peninsula Medical School
Sue Locke
Senior Coordinator (Admissions)
Peninsula College of Medicine and Dentistry
John Bull Building
Tamar Science Park
Research Way
Plymouth PL6 8BU
Tel: 01752 437334
Email: sue.locke@pms.ac.uk
Web: www.pms.ac.uk

Queen Mary (Barts and the London)
Miss Moushumi Bhowmik
Events Administrator (Student Recruitment and Admissions)
Barts and the London School of Medicine and Dentistry
Garrod Building
Turner Street
London E1 2AD
Tel: 020 7882 8478
Email: medicaladmissions@qmul.ac.uk
Web: www.smd.qmul.ac.uk

Queen's Belfast
S. Wisener
Admissions Officer
Queen's University Belfast
Belfast BT7 1NN
Northern Ireland
Web: www.qub.ac.uk/cm

Saint Andrews
Mary Ainsworth
Admissions Officer
University of St Andrews
Admissions Application Centre
St Katharine's West
16 The Scores
St Andrews KY16 9AX
Tel: 0133 4463593
Email: medadmiss@st-andrews.ac.uk
Web: http://medicine.st-andrews.ac.uk

Saint George's
Caroline Persaud
Admissions Officer
St George's Hospital School of Medicine
Cranmer Terrace
London SW17 0RE
Web: www.sgul.ac.uk

Sheffield
Joanne Marshall
Medical Admissions Officer
Faculty of Medicine
Beech Hill Road
Sheffield S10 2RX
Email: medadmissions@sheffield.ac.uk
Web: www.shef.ac.uk/medicine

Southampton
Dr Jenny Skidmore
Admissions Tutor
School of Medicine
Biomedical Sciences Building
Bassett Crescent East
Southampton SO16 7PX
Web: www.som.soton.ac.uk

Swansea
Admissions Office
School of Medicine
Grove Building
University of Wales, Swansea
Singleton Park
Swansea SA2 8PP
Web: www.medicine.swan.ac.uk

UCL (and Royal Free)
Dr Caroline Aspinwall
Principal Admissions Officer
The Medical School
University College London
Gower Street
London WC1E 6BT
Tel: 0207 679 0868
Web: www.ucl.ac.uk/medicalschool

Warwick
Lesley Ling
Senior Admissions Assistant
University House
University of Warwick
Coventry CV4 8UW
Email: Lara.McCarthy@warwick.ac.uk
Web: www2.warwick.ac.uk/fac/med
Note: Warwick is graduate entry only university, not A levels entry.

Access to Medicine
The College of West Anglia
Derek Holmes
Tennyson Avenue
King's Lynn PE30 2QW
Tel: 01553 761144 (ext 309)
Web: www.col-westanglia.ac.uk/atm-apply

Studying outside the UK

M&D Europe (UK) Ltd
(for English-language courses in the Czech Republic and the Cayman Islands)
616 Mitcham Road
Croydon CR0 3AA
Tel: 0871 717 1291 or +44 (0) 870 487 1785 (from outside the UK)
Web: www.studymedicine.co.uk

Royal College of Surgeons in Ireland
123 St Stephen's Green
Dublin 2
Ireland
Web: www.rcsi.ie

Saint George's University School of Medicine
Margaret Lambert
University Centre
Grenada
West Indies
Tel: 0800 169 9061 (from the UK)
www.sgu.edu

Volunteering

Positive East
(HIV/AIDS volunteering)
159 Mile End Road
London E1 4AQ
Web: www.positiveeast.org.uk

■ Tables

Table 7 Medical school statistics for 2009 entry

	Applied	Interviews	Offers	Accepted
Aberdeen	~1,450	643	426	182
Birmingham	2,649	891	822	372
Brighton & Sussex	2,700[1]	484[2]	232	140
Bristol	~3,000	~750	295	216
Cambridge	1,702	Not available	290	276
Grad entry	155	Not available	34	23
Cardiff	2,610	946	450	356

	Applied	Interviews	Offers	Accepted
Dundee	1,326	445	340	159
Durham	As Newcastle			
East Anglia A100[3]	1,319	500	308	143
East Anglia A104[4]	310	60		24
Edinburgh	2,424	36	392	225
Glasgow	~1,700	~800	~450	223[5]
Hull York	1,034	594	352	146
Imperial	2,500	721	490	326
Keele	1,210	400	265	137
King's	~3,500	~1,000	~640	320
Leeds	3,660	~600	400	223
Leicester	~1,600	~900	450	200
Liverpool	~2,025	~1,088	~781	295
Manchester	2,255	939	780	393
Newcastle	2,715	1,179	600	380
Nottingham	2,138	840	506	249
Oxford	~1,300	425[6]	160[7]	153
Peninsula	2,196	671	394	212
Queen Mary	2,367	876	617	280
Queen's Belfast	~750	~40	~360	261
St Andrews	987	532	320	152
St George's	1,519	800	342	188
Sheffield	2,591	650	481	252
Southampton	2,727	231	419	209
UCL	2,743	669	447	327

1| Applications number is for the 2010 cycle thus numbers incomplete.
2| These numbers are still the 2009 cycle.
3| A100 Medicine 5FT Hon.
4| A104 Medicine with a Foundation Year.
5| 18 places available for non EU students.
6| Oxford always interviews 425 applicants despite number of cohort.
7| 4 deferred entry.
Note: Figures for graduate-entry programmes are excluded. These can be found on www.mpw.co.uk/getintomed.

Table 8 Medical school admissions policies for 2009/10 entry

Institution	Usual offer	Usual AS requirements	Usual A2 requirements	Retakes considered*
Aberdeen	AAB	none	Chem + 1 other science/Maths	No
Birmingham	AAA	B in Biol	Chem + 1 other science/Maths	In extenuating circumstances and if narrowly missed AAA
Brighton & Sussex	AAA or A*AB	A in AS Biol if not taken at A level	Biol/Chem (A grades)	In extenuating circumstances and if narrowly missed AAA
Bristol	AAB	4 separate subjects to have been studied	Chemistry (A grade) + 1 other lab-based science (one of Human Biol, Biol or Physics)	In extenuating circumstances
Cambridge	A*AA	3rd science/Maths	Chem + 1 other science/Maths	In extenuating circumstances
Cardiff	AAB	Biol + Chem; A in Biol/Chem if not at A2	Biol/Chem	If previously applied to Cardiff
Dundee	AAA	Biol	Chem + 1 other science/Maths	In extenuating circumstances
Durham	Same as for Newcastle			
East Anglia A100	AAB Access encouraged	B in 4th AS	Biol	Yes but must achieve A grades
East Anglia A104	BCC	No AS requirement	No usual requirements	Resits not accepted
Edinburgh	AAA	Biol; B in 4th AS	Chem + 1 other science	In extenuating circumstances
Glasgow*	AAB	Biol	Chem + 1 other science/Maths + B in GCSE English	In extenuating circumstances
Hull York	AAB	B in 4th AS	Biol + Chem (AA)	In extenuating circumstances
Imperial	AAA	B in 4th AS	Biol/Chem	In extenuating circumstances and if previously applied to Imperial
Keele	AAB	Chem or Biol; B at GCSE in non-AS sciences	Biol/Chem + 1 other science/Maths	Yes – see prospectus
King's	AAA	Biol + Chem; grade B	Biol/Chem	In extenuating circumstances
Leeds	AAB	Not specified	Chem grade A	In extenuating circumstances

Leicester	AAB	Biol	Chem	In extenuating circumstances and if previously held Leicester offer
Liverpool*	AAB (A Biology A Chem)	B in 4th AS (Gen St or Crit Think accepted)	Biol + Chem + 3rd + 4th AS	In extenuating circumstances
Manchester	AAA	4 AS subjects excluding General Studies	Chemistry + 1 other science	No
Newcastle	AAA	If only one of Biol and Chem at A2/AS, other at GCSE	Biol/Chem	In extenuating circumstances
Nottingham	AAB	AA in Biol + Chem	Biol + Chem + 1 other	In extenuating circumstances
Oxford†	AAA	Not specified	Chemistry, + Biology and/or Physics and/or Maths	See advice on our website
Peninsula	AAB	B in 4th AS	A in 1 science	Yes
Queen Mary	AAA	B in 4th AS and B in either Chem or Biol AS	Two must be Sciences either Biol or Chem	No‡
Queen's Belfast	AAA	Biol; A in 4th AS	Chem + 1 other science/Maths	If previously held Queen's offer and missed by 1 grade
St Andrews	AAB	GCSE Biol + Maths if not AS/A2	Chem + 1 other science/Maths	In extenuating circumstances
St George's	AAA–BBC	Biol + Chem; B in 4th AS	Biol/Chem	No
Sheffield	AAB	Chem + other science	AB in Chem + 1 other Science/ Maths	No
Southampton	AAB	B in Chem/Biol	Biol/Chem	In extenuating circumstances and if retaking one subject
UCL	AAA	B in Biol	Chem and Biology	No

* Retake candidates will normally be expected to achieve AAA.

† Oxford offers two courses:

  1| A100 a 6 year course in medicine (graduates may apply and complete this course in 5 years. Contact address: Administrative Officer, Medical Sciences Teaching Centre, South Parks Road, Oxford OX1 3PL; tel 01865 285783; email admissions@medschool.ox.ac.uk

  2| A101 a 4 year accelerated course (for graduates in experimental sciences). Contact address: Medical Sciences Office, John Radcliffe Hospital, Headington, Oxford OX3 9DU; tel 01865 228975; email lesley.maitland@medsci.ox.ac.uk

‡ Queen Mary also takes into account GCSE grades. It expects applicants to offer a wide range of subjects with at least six at grade A or B. English Language, Mathematics and science subjects are all required at grade B.

Note: Details were correct when going to press – check websites for updated information.

Table 9 Interview and written test policies for 2009 entry

	Typical length	No.	Panel members[1]	Test
Aberdeen	20 mins	2	ABCDFGH	UKCAT
Birmingham	15 mins	3	BCDEFG	10 min thinking test
Brighton & Sussex	20 mins	3	ECDFGJ	UKCAT
Bristol	15 mins	2	ABCDFGH	None
Cambridge	2 × 20 mins	2–3	BCDFG	BMAT
Cardiff	20 mins	2–3	ABCDEFGJ	UKCAT
Dundee	10 × 7 mins		CDEJ	UKCAT
Durham	45 mins	2	CDFJK	UKCAT
East Anglia A100	45 mins	7[2]	ABCDFG	UKCAT; case history to discuss
East Anglia A104		2	BFG	
Edinburgh	30 mins	6	G	UKCAT
Glasgow	15 mins	2	ACDFG	UKCAT
Hull York	20 mins	2	CF	UKCAT; short article to comment on
Imperial	15 mins	4	BCEFG	BMAT
Keele	20 mins	3	DFK	UKCAT
King's	15 mins	2	BCDF	UKCAT; 20 min questionnaire
Leeds	20 mins	3	ABCDEFGHIJ	UKCAT
Leicester	15 mins	2	CE	UKCAT
Liverpool	15 mins	2	ACDFGI	None
Manchester	60 mins	3	CDFGH	UKCAT
Newcastle	25–30 mins	2	ABCDFGHIJ	UKCAT
Nottingham[3]	15 mins	2	ABCDFGH	UKCAT
Oxford	2 × 20–30 mins	2–4	CF	BMAT (for course A100)
Peninsula	20 mins	3–4	DFHJ	UKCAT; 20 min questionnaire GAMSAT for graduates and mature students
Queen Mary	15 mins	3	ABCDEFGHJ	UKCAT; video
Queen's Belfast	15 mins	3	DFH	UKCAT
St Andrews	20 mins	2	ABCDFGHJ	UKCAT
St George's	15–20 mins	4	ABCDEFGHJ	UKCAT
Sheffield	20 mins	3	CDEFGIJK	UKCAT
Southampton	20 mins	2	ABCDFGHJ	UKCAT
UCL	15–20 mins	3	ABCDEFGHJK	BMAT

1| A = admissions dean/associate dean; B = admissions tutor; C = doctor from medical school; D = doctor from local area; E = medical student; F = member of academic staff; G = member of admissions committee; H = administrator; I = member of trust board; J = other healthcare professional; K = lay person

2| Each interviewer has 5 minutes with candidate.

3| Nottingham offers two courses – A100 (the details for this course are shown above), and A101 graduate entry medicine which is a 4 year programme, open to graduates who have achieved a 2:2 in their first degree. These applicants must sit the GAMSAT exam. Contact details for this course are GEM@nottingham.ac.uk.

Postscript

If you have any comments or questions arising from this book, the staff of MPW and I would be very happy to answer them. You can contact us at the address given below.

Good luck with your application to medical school!

Steven Piumatti
MPW (London)
90/92 Queen's Gate
London SW7 5AB
Tel: 020 7835 1355
Fax: 020 7225 2953
Email: enquiries@mpw.co.uk

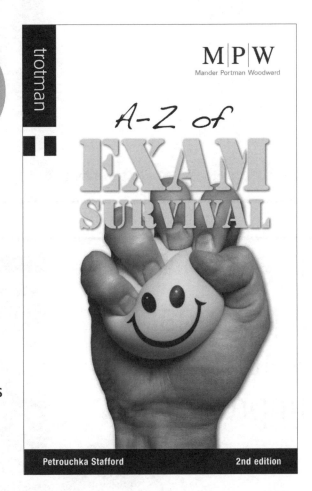